A Question of RESPECT

Praise for
A Question of RESPECT

"It is entirely fitting that Ed Goeas and Celinda Lake, two of the nation's premier pollsters and founders of the Battleground Poll, a bipartisan project that has survived and thrived during three decades of worsening polarization, would together write such a wise and thoughtful book as *"A Question of Respect: Bringing Us Together in a Deeply Divided Nation."* For Goeas, a Republican, and Lake, a Democrat, deepening partisan hostility is a constant presence in the work they do for candidates, advocacy groups, political parties, and other clients. Both authors understand the corrosive forces that have so weakened the pillars of democracy, and together they have produced a substantive strategy to pull the system out of a nosedive to disaster. This book provides sustenance and encouragement to both the political expert and the ordinary voter whose faith in politics has been sorely tested."

Thomas B. Edsall,
New York Times columnist

"Bringing Us Together in a Deeply Divided Nation" is a herculean task—massive in scope and in its expectation, yet fundamental to the survival of our democracy. Who better to address this threat than the team of Celinda Lake, a woman of intelligence and integrity, and Ed Goeas, a man of principle and purpose? Each brings a nuanced perspective to the reader that elicits thoughtful discussions and a call to action – to respect one another. Politically, it affirms there is no other way to preserve and maintain the United States of America. Personally, it is a nod to empathy — the connective tissue in our humanity. When we embrace empathy, we will be on our way to fixing what has been broken—trust in the ideals and values of America. It is indeed *A Question of Respect."*

Valerie Biden Owens,
Campaign strategist and author
of the *NY Times* best-selling book *Growing Up Biden*

"With over 30 years of successfully working together despite their political differences, Ed Goeas and Celinda Lake are the ideal two people to explain not only how we got into this mess, but how we can get out of it. Their careers are a vivid testimony to the ability of people with divergent views to thrive in partnership. And this brilliant book is testimony to the sorts of things that people can accomplish working together through their differences. Ed and Celinda cite respect as the key ingredient in the elixir that can heal our fractured nation. This timely and important book earned my respect, and I'm sure it will earn yours."

Donna Brazile,
Former chair, Democratic National Committee

"Ed Goeas is not only a premier pollster, but he is very savvy about strategy, operations, and tactics. I've used him many times, and he is as good as it gets in his profession. His continued work with Celinda Lake at Georgetown University's Institute of Politics & Public Service, and their writing of this book together, is a testament to the great things that can be accomplished when people on opposites sides of the political spectrum work collaboratively, thoughtfully, and most important—respectfully. *A Question of Respect: Bringing Us Together in a Deeply Divided Nation* reminds us of a very important lesson: that we can disagree without being disagreeable. Politicos and people everywhere can learn a lot from this book. Instruction on civility couldn't be more significant—now more than ever before."

Governor Haley Barbour,
Governor of Mississippi 2004–2012,
Former chair Republican National Committee

"As the story was told and retold on the House floor, Franklin was walking out of Independence Hall after the Constitutional Convention in 1787 when someone shouted out, "Doctor, what have we got, A Republic or a Monarchy?" to which Franklin supposedly responded: "A Republic if you can keep it." In the easy-to-read new book, *A Question of Respect*, noted bi-partisan pollsters Celinda Lake and Ed Goeas reflect on today's societal fractures, the causes, and effects of our broken state of politics/government, and the actions necessary to preserve this experiment in self-government known as the American Republic. Rich in substance, this must-read book is timely and important for anyone who values freedom and longs for a political and cultural landscape free of today's dangerous acrimony."

Zach Wamp,
Member of Congress 1995–2011

"Many of us—grizzled veterans of Capitol Hill and political novices alike—yearn for more thoughtful and effective governance of our democracy. Now comes a blueprint for breaking through the deeply partisan gridlock currently afflicting our national, state and local political landscapes. Drawing from their decades of polling experience and bi-partisan partnership, Ed and Celinda astutely provide the diagnosis AND prescribe the cure for what ails us—and it starts with respect. Filled with anecdotes, data, lived experiences, and personal introspection, *A Question of Respect* inspires and gives us hope for a better way forward. I am heartened by the optimism that shines through in this book, and eager for our political class to apply its lessons!"

James Conzelman,
President/CEO, Ripon Society and Franklin Center
for Global Policy Exchange

"John Kennedy joked that Washington is a town of Southern efficiency and Northern charm. I believe it is most fortunate and encouraging that, even in this moment of high political temperature and low behavior, some people are able to successfully work together across the partisan divide. In this remarkable book, *A Question of Respect*, Republic-based Ed Goeas and Democrat-based Celinda Lake, who have been polling partners and friends for decades, use lessons learned from their bi-partisan immersion. Taking the public's temperature in their highly respected joint Battleground Polls, they are uniquely able to diagnose our current civic ailments—and prescribe cures."

George F. Will,
Author and columnist for *The Washington Post*

"While our politics and the campaigns that shape them are growing more turbulent and intense, there is no one better suited to diagnose what is driving this phenomenon, and how to bridge the divide, than elections veterans like Ed and Celinda. They speak with authority and expertise on public opinion because they have dedicated their entire careers to understanding it. In my own experience, Ed has been a trusted advisor who not only talks about restoring our country's civic life to a healthy, vibrant, condition – he lives it. I can't recommend highly enough the framework he and Celinda provide here to mend our public discourse."

Senator John Boozman,
Arkansas

"Anyone who has spent any significant portion of their life enmeshed in American politics knows that the tenor of today's political debate--the viciousness, the contempt, the anger--has plummeted to a new depth. There's simply no way our country will address its biggest challenges if Democrats and Republicans are more inclined to undermine one another than to solve real problems together. In *A Question of Respect*, two people who really know the ins and outs of Washington unpack what's gone wrong and how we might right the ship. Every challenge we face today as a nation depends on our finding a solution to this problem first. If you want to understand the underlying dynamics, read this book."

Nancy Jacobson,
CEO & Founder No Labels
Helped establish Problem Solvers Caucus

"Our democracy is facing a crisis. At a time when a growing number of Americans are losing faith in government, politics, and the media, *A Question of Respect: Bringing us Together in a Deeply Divided Nation* offers a comprehensive blueprint for restoring confidence in the institutions that are the very fabric of our democracy. With the expertise of Ed Goeas and Celinda Lake—two political veterans who understand the nuances of messaging and media in our politics—this book offers a keen understanding of how we reached this point and some of the key figures responsible. Historically, our country was forged on fierce debate, followed by compromise for the common good. Ed and Celinda chronicle the seismic changes in our politics from the 2nd half of the 20th century through today, while also giving us hope that our politics can move to a better place. Now more than ever, this book is vitally important."

Steve Scully,
Senior VP Bipartisan Policy Center
Host, "The Briefing" Sirius XM POTUS

"Civility is disappearing faster than the rainforests, and with it goes respect, which. once gone, leaves both politics and humanity defenseless, naked and nothing short of barbaric. This book sets out a compelling non-partisan blueprint to keeping barbarism at bay. Ed Goeas is a gifted humanist who, along with Celinda Lake, has managed to build an instructive bridge between the unfamiliar analytical world of political polling and the everyday man and woman's need for civility and desire for respect."

Bianca Goodloe
Entertainment Lawyer
Adjunct Professor of media and film studies at UCLA

"The Republican pollster and campaign strategist and the Democratic pollster, long-time professional collaborators, clearly respect each other's differing ideologies. At a perfect time for our country, and perhaps the world-at-large, Ed and Celinda have co-authored *A Question of RESPECT*. Their purpose: "bringing us together in a deeply divided nation" as their subtitle states. May their wisdom help override our foolishness. I strongly suggest—okay, I urge you—to read this book."

Speaker John Boehner
2011-2015

"What's respect got to do with it? Everything, Democratic pollster Celinda Lake and Republican strategist Ed Goeas argue in their provocative new book. After a 30-year partnership in polling across party lines, they dissect what has made many American voters so cynical—and vulnerable to anti-democratic appeals—and how they can be reached today. Essential reading in our nation's divided time."

Susan Page,
Washington Bureau Chief, *USA Today* author,
Madam Speaker: Nancy Pelosi and the Lessons of Power

"Anyone who wants to understand the divisions facing our country will be well served by a close reading of *A Question of Respect*. Individually, Celinda and Ed are two of the smartest pollsters in the game. Together they've given us a roadmap for understanding the essential factors threatening our democracy, and a valuable tool for setting ourselves towards a brighter, more stable future."

Maria Teresa Kumar
Emmy-nominated, MSNBC contributor
President and CEO of Voto Latino

"Change is coming in America. Some fiercely resist it; others hopefully embrace it. All of us are uncertain about what's ahead. Rancor and violence in our discourse and deeds make the mood ugly to find consensus. Perilous times, indeed. Authors Ed Goeas and Celinda Lake focus on how we got here and how we might move forward to better days. Their wide-ranging political backgrounds and extensive experience analyzing a myriad of challenges that confront our policy makers qualify them to credibly address possibilities for more comity and effective result in our national debate.

I grew up in New England in the WWII / early Cold War era. Common courtesy was the norm; good manners were expected. Disrespectful behavior or speech were unthinkable in our household—and would have ended in swift scolding. Fast forward to the start of the 21st Century: President Obama ran on a promise that his administration would bring "fundamental change" to America. In his State of The Union address he identified and deplored "the crisis of confidence" in people's trust of government. He was right – change and crisis have been intensifying ever since. Obama is not to blame. We all are.

I do not agree with several of the posits of Ed and Celinda's book, but I know I could have a pleasant and reasoned discussion about our differences. And I applaud them for directing their audiences to reopen the doorways to respect."

Porter J. Goss
Former SW Florida Congressman
Former Director of the CIA

"Many outside Washington's Beltway or west of the Hudson River may be tempted to see this as an "Acela Corridor" book. That's wrong. Like Ed, I'm a former political warrior turned champion for civil discourse and have gone from being part of the problem to, hopefully, being part of the solution. Partisans and tribalists today are more interested in exploiting issues for political, even personal gain, not resolving them. Ed and Celinda expertly model and outline how *trust must be built*, resulting in respect, and in the process rediscovering pathways to meaningful bipartisan communication and cooperation without sacrificing core principles and values."

Kelly D. Johnston
Former Secretary of the US Senate (1995-96)

"As a very willing player in today's partisan style of journalism and politics, I had given up thinking about the return to respect, compromise and even unity. Washington's power pollsters Ed Goeas and Celinda Lake call for in '*A Question of Respect.*' It seemed to me that when people talk about compromise, what they really mean is 'Agree with me!' Just say 'no' and move on is the answer for most. But in providing a roadmap to respect and bipartisanship, liberal Lake and conservative Goeas offer up a very personal lesson for all of us on the final page. In acknowledging how their politically divided relationship changed over the two-year writing project, they basically said that time and listening were the best medicine. 'We still have areas of disagreement. We always will. But we will always hear each other out.' It's often the simple solutions that seem hardest to find. Theirs is not only a cure for what ails Washington, but maybe the salve to our divided nation, packed in a powerful and concise read. Bravo."

Paul Bedard,
Washington Secrets columnist for the Washington Examiner

"Ed Goeas and Celinda Lake have spent thirty years successfully working across party lines and philosophical differences. Their work has required patience, debate, compromise and, above all, respect for each other. This is the way things used to work in Washington, before some leaders in both parties decided that the ends justified the means and that compromise was a sign of weakness. This book will help well-intentioned leaders of both parties understand the root of our dysfunction and motivate them to work with their opponents—starting by respecting them. John McCain would have loved this book."

Charlie Black
Chief Strategist, McCain 08

"The political landscape today is monumentally different from when I first entered public service decades ago. I have worked with Ed for over half of my career. While his success is about strategy, timing and tactics, it's as much about his genuine care and passion for helping people. His love for our nation is clearly evident. As I learned throughout my career, major change will upset some people, but if you want to accomplish things for the greater good, you must be bold enough to take steps to do what is right, no matter the personal sacrifice. Ed and Celinda have been bold in their assessment of our divided nation as it sits today, which may make some people uncomfortable. Both have earned the respect of their political parties. This book and their needed insight provide a path for us to renew our faith in our nation and our system of government."

Oklahoma Governor Mary Fallin
2011-2019

"Ed and Celinda have revealed the heart of Americans - their desire for civility and compromise - and offered data to back it up affirming what so many of us intuitively know as patriots. This provides an incredibly valuable blueprint for all of us, especially those of us working to advance structural reforms to change the way we currently incentivize our elected officials. This is no surprise as Ed and Celinda have spent their careers listening to Americans"

Lindsey Drath
Unite America and Longtime GOP Operative

"Time and time again, from candidates' living rooms to corporate boardrooms, and from State Houses to the halls of Congress, candidates, elected officials, their advisors and donors struggle to figure out "what's happening." More often than not, if they are smart, people say -- "Call Ed!" or "What does Celinda say?" For years, I have looked forward to the results of Celinda's and Ed's non-partisan polling collaboration. In this book they present their honest, undistilled, and refreshing analysis of the problems facing our country along with some intriguing possible solutions -- even when they don't agree. Reading this book is also a joy because of the behind-the-scenes look the authors afford us into their many years of helping to guide the leaders of our country."

Brian Baker
Advisor to the Ricketts Family

"This powerfully optimistic, aspirational book will provoke readers—in and out of professional politics—to a realistic reflection on how we got to, and how we can walk back from, the political abyss currently plaguing all communities. In "popping the filter bubble" for decades, churning out zero sum counterproductive policy puffery favored by a myopic, elite, exclusive, detached, dystopian micro minority, Ed and Celinda provide a forward path for a much-needed political course correction premised on timeless truths: respect and results. They practiced what they preach to produce their collective tour de force. Constricting themselves to a "we" voice, with respectful open minds and generous hearts, while eschewing today's hyper-histrionic hash tag intellectually and morally bereft pseudo politics, reflecting on their own long, distinct and distinguished experiences in front line foxholes across the globe, the outcome is an illuminating, clear-eyed, contemporary history of our best and worst attempts at E Pluribus Unum, which arrives at a no nonsense, common sense course of reset recommendations to root out the profane and usher in productive, inclusive political and policy progress. A very good book by very good people about a very good country in very bad times. I could not put it down. Get copies for everyone you know, especially those with whom you've stopped communicating!"

Mary Matalin,
American political consultant

"During World War II's bitter Pacific campaign, Admiral William "Bull" Halsey had the slogan "Kill Japs. Kill Japs. Kill More Japs." Posted on large billboards for every sailor to see. In most wars, both sides seek to dehumanize their foe to inspire their own forces to destroy them. It works. But the process also produces deeply held animosities that increase the ferocity of combat, and make the inevitable need for negotiation and reconciliation more difficult. Similar dynamics are at work in American society, most notably our politics, and that is why A Question of Respect is so important. Ed and Celinda, two experienced veterans of political combat have written a thoughtful examination of where the problems lie, and what we can do about them. It's not a solution, that's up to us, but it's an invaluable roadmap that each of us should carry."

General Stan McChrystal (Ret.)
President/CEO The McChrystal Group

A Question of RESPECT

Bringing Us Together in a Deeply Divided Nation

ED GOEAS

CELINDA LAKE

NEW YORK

LONDON • NASHVILLE • MELBOURNE • VANCOUVER

A Question of RESPECT

Bringing Us Together in a Deeply Divided Nation

Published in New York, New York, by Morgan James Publishing. Morgan James is a trademark of Morgan James, LLC. www.MorganJamesPublishing.com

Proudly distributed by Ingram Publisher Services.

A **FREE** ebook edition is available for you
or a friend with the purchase of this print book.

CLEARLY SIGN YOUR NAME ABOVE

Instructions to claim your free ebook edition:
1. Visit MorganJamesBOGO.com
2. Sign your name CLEARLY in the space above
3. Complete the form and submit a photo
   of this entire page
4. You or your friend can download the ebook
   to your preferred device

ISBN 9781636980409 paperback
ISBN 9781636980416 ebook
Library of Congress Control Number:
2022944970

Cover & Interior Design by:
Christopher Kirk
www.GFSstudio.com

Morgan James is a proud partner of Habitat for Humanity Peninsula
and Greater Williamsburg. Partners in building since 2006.

Get involved today! Visit MorganJamesPublishing.com/giving-back

To Senator John McCain—a true leader. John lit the way for me as a shining example of a politician modeling respect and civility at its best, both between political parties and the people.

Also, for the five Georgetown University students who made up my Student Strategy Group for the Fellowship in Civility that I led in the fall of 2018.

John McCain and these young leaders of tomorrow gave me hope for our nation's future and inspired me to author this book with Celinda. (Ed Goeas)

Table of Contents

Acknowledgments
from Ed Goeas

F irst, my wonderfully smart and loving wife Lisa and our children, Emma, Robert, and Bennett. They are the foundation on which all else rests. They are each unique in their own way, but they also have a common bond in that they each stole my heart and made my life complete.

My older daughter, Jenn Street, who has not only been a great sister to Emma, Robert, and Bennett but played a key role in their lives as a teacher/educator.

My father, Ed Jr. (I am the third), was a true patriot and philosopher. Over the years, I find myself quoting the lessons he taught me about the importance of mutual respect. My mother, Nancy, who repeatedly kept our family together while my father went off to war. Not an easy task with four young boys—which I am sure, at times, felt like her own personal war zone.

In putting together and building the Tarrance Group, my partners, Dave Sackett and Brian Tringali, over the last thirty-five years became more like brothers than business partners. We not only saw our company grow but our families grow and, in many cases, grow up and start their own families.

Then there is my other political partner from across the aisle, Celinda Lake. I cannot say enough good about her. Just about the time I believed the bar of respect and friendship could not go any higher, there she was, moving it up a couple more notches. She was the perfect co-author for this book because while there are numerous issues we differ on, when it comes to character, Celinda's civility, trust, and respect certainly puts her at the front of each of those lines.

Eddie Mahe, Nancy Dwight, and Joe Gaylord, who all played a significant role in encouraging me to take the career path I did, and at the national level. I do not believe any of these three pioneers of modern-day campaigns will ever get full credit for what they did in bringing in younger, talented men and women who have truly strengthened the Republican Party for decades.

My Friday morning Bible study group at The Royal Restaurant in Alexandria, Virginia, with whom I have met with over the last fifteen years—Charlie Black, Robin Roberts, Bill Harris, Dennis Whitfield, Ed Stewart, Bill Greener, and Bill Lee. Thank you one and all for keeping faith as a beautiful and enriching common bond, both spiritually and politically.

Then there is Ed Rollins. We have been friends ever since we first met, while he was serving as political director of the Reagan White House and I was political director of the National Republican Congressional Committee. Rollins never forgot his blue-collar upbringing and always brought it to every political discussion. A dose of reality that was both noteworthy and worth its weight in gold.

Many thanks to our book collaborators, Judy Katz and Kai Flanders. Your editorial guidance and supervision helped make the book writing process both productive and enjoyable. Kudos to you for your mastery.

I want to acknowledge those candidates I have been blessed to work with and for through the years—from the early days with Frank Keating to Congressmen John Hiler, Porter Goss, and Zach Wamp, among others, to Senators James Lankford, John Boozman, and Joni Ernst, and Governors Mary Fallin, John Kasich, Scott Walker, and Haley Barbour. And of course, there was John McCain's presidential race, where I was privileged to serve as a political advisor and play a key role in his 2008 convention.

Thank you to the Morgan James Publishing team for supporting our venture.

I call myself blessed because about the time the ugliness of the political arena began to beat me down, someone special would come along who was there for all the right reasons. They would be authentically committed to keeping democracy alive by focusing on the needs of the American people, not on political power. As Governor Haley Barbour used to say, "Keeping the main thing . . . *the main thing!*"

Acknowledgments from Celinda Lake

I want to acknowledge my parents, Alice and Jack Lake. Like Ed's parents they had a foundational influence on my values and the perspective I bring to this joint endeavor. They fundamentally believed in the value of and respect for every human being—no matter their station in life, who they are, what they look like, or where they live. They valued working together and individual freedom—and found a home for that in moving from New York City to a ranch in Montana in 1948. I also want to acknowledge my brother, Jackson, who always supported my decisions, even when my parents might disagree.

I want to acknowledge my friends who have been like my family. They have picked me up when I was down, dusted me off, and got me back in the saddle, as we say in Montana, and then have been there to celebrate the good times and victories. Among the best of my friends has been Ed Goeas. He has always been there, and it has been a great privilege to do this joint journey and endeavor with him, to see his vision and guiding principles reflected in this book.

I want to acknowledge my partners in LRP—Alysia Snell, David Mermin, Daniel Gotoff, Joshua Ulibarri, Jonathan Voss, Bob Meadows, and Robert Wesley. None of this would have happened without them. I am so appreciative of the principled, strategic, and important work we have done, separately and together. I also want to thank the amazing staff we have had over the years. I especially want to thank the team who helped with this book: Michael Murphy, Sandra Markowitz, Mac Pugh, and Ronan Ferrentino. They also were instrumental—along with the students of Georgetown—to bring the voices of the next generations to the end of this book.

I am eternally grateful for the incredible clients we have had, both issue and candidates. We have shared a decades-long fight for our values, for change, and for people. I wake up every morning so admiring of what they do and so proud and appreciative of having been part of their teams and their important work.

I also express gratitude to Morgan James Publishing for helping us take our message far and wide.

I want to add my thanks to our collaborators, Judy Katz and Kai Flanders. Your guidance, expertise, and energy have been so important to this book. And Ed and I both want to thank Mo Elleithee for his tremendously valuable insights, especially when he had so much on his plate!

Foreword

For most of my adult life, I was a political hack.

For twenty years, I worked as a campaign press secretary and communications strategist. I worked for four presidential candidates, numerous candidates for the Senate and governor, was the chief spokesperson for the Democratic Party, and advised several progressive interest groups and Super PACs. I've been a partisan talking-head on cable television and written more than a few scripts for negative ads.

I was a hard-hitting political operative, and I was pretty good at it. I once bumped into a national political reporter I knew at an event for one of my candidates, and he told me he was excited to hear that I had joined the campaign because he knew it would mean there would be "blood on the walls." For years, I considered that a compliment.

I shouldn't have. The dirty secret is that many of the candidates I worked against I actually respected. As much as I disagreed with their politics, they were stepping up to the plate, putting their names on the ballot, and taking the hits in the same way my candidate was. I didn't agree with them on very much, but I respected their motives. Sure, there were some genuinely bad apples, but most of them were there for the right reason. They wanted to serve the public.

Still, that didn't stop me from hitting them hard. The press releases I wrote were snarky, mean, and often downright nasty. That's how I learned to do it. Like many of my peers, I believed that was necessary if we wanted to win. It was part of the game. The problem was people hated the game the way it was being played. I spent two decades doing all of the things people say they hate about politics, and I had become part of the problem.

It's not just government. People have lost faith in most institutions—not just politics and government—but also Wall Street, traditional and mainstream media, academia, and many others. And this is true across the globe. According to the 2022 Edelman "Trust Barometer," a global survey of 35,000 respondents across twenty-eight countries, nearly one in two respondents view government and media as divisive forces in society. And approximately two-thirds of people globally believe journalists (67 percent), government leaders (66 percent), and business executives (63 percent) are "purposely trying to mislead people by saying things they know are false or gross exaggerations."[1]

Of course, we shouldn't be surprised. American voters have been telling us this for decades. In the wake of Watergate and the Vietnam War, voters responded to Jimmy Carter in 1976 because he was a political outsider. Four years later, frustrated with inflation and the twin crises of energy and Americans being held hostage in Iran, they turned to another outsider in Ronald Reagan. In 1992, at a time when people believed conservatives were only looking out for the wealthy, and liberals were just focused on the poor, Bill Clinton won on the message of "Fighting for the forgotten middle class."

In 2008, Barack Obama's themes of "hope and change" spoke to an electorate frustrated by a system they believed was stacked against average Americans by special interests.

One year later, two seemingly opposed movements in the Tea Party and the Occupy Movement arose simultaneously with similar messages: Wall Street and Washington were in cahoots and the average citizen was getting squeezed out. And in 2015, Donald Trump tapped into people's anger, saying the *entire system* was rigged, portraying himself as the ultimate outsider willing to do and say anything to blow it all up. Today, the frustration grows, and the polarization along with it. People don't feel these institutions are serving them anymore. They don't feel seen or heard. They don't feel *respected*.

Now, I'm not mourning the loss of some mythical bygone era, where political leaders worked together in harmony. Politics in America has *always* been a contact sport. There have been times when it's been worse. We've had one non-partisan president in the history of the Republic, and in the race to succeed him, John Adams and Thomas Jefferson called each other liars, thieves, scoundrels, and worse. A former Treasury secretary was killed in a duel by a sitting vice president. A sitting member of the House savagely beat a sitting senator with a cane on the floor of the United States Senate.

We went to war with ourselves over whether we should keep fellow human beings in bondage. Japanese-Americans were put in internment camps during the Second World War. Violence erupted between protesters and police outside of national political conventions. College students were killed by the National Guard on a college campus during a protest against the Vietnam War. A future member of Congress had his skull cracked by state troopers during a peaceful Civil Rights march.

And yet, despite our history, today's political polarization feels as bad as it has ever been. Recent polling conducted by the authors shows that a majority of Americans believe our political divisions are so strong, we are approaching civil war. Something has to change.

So, in the summer of 2015, I stepped off the partisan battlefield to launch the Institute of Politics and Public Service at my alma mater, Georgetown University. I wanted to explore how we got to this point and, more importantly, work with young people to figure out ways to do it better. A primary focus of our efforts is to pop the filter bubbles that so many of us live in, bringing together people with divergent views to better understand one another as we explore the big political issues of the day. Our belief is that better conversations are an important step toward better solutions.

It was here that I began working with Ed Goeas and Celinda Lake. I had been familiar with the work of these two legendary pollsters—one a Republican and the other a Democrat—for decades. They have been working together for nearly thirty years on their famous "Battleground Poll," in which their partisan firms jointly conduct a survey testing voter attitudes on key issues and then write separate analyses to help the press make sense of the data from their different perspectives. They, and their polls, demonstrate how people from very different points on the political spectrum could collaborate for the public good, and even develop a friendship along the way.

So I was thrilled when Ed, after completing a semester-long fellowship at our Institute in 2018, in which he worked with students to explore civility in politics, approached me about making us the new home for the Battleground Poll. As my conversations with Ed and Celinda progressed, we became excited about expanding the scope of the polling with a new element—an entire segment that would track voter attitudes toward civility in politics over time. We would explore how bad voters thought it was, who they blamed, and how much they really wanted it.

Launched in 2019 as a companion to the Battleground Poll, the Georgetown Institute of Politics and Public Service *Civility Poll* has shown fascinating results. People are worried about the state of our national discourse. They are concerned that we are headed toward violence (even before the Capitol Insurrection of January 6, 2021). They blame political leaders of both parties, the media, social media companies, and special interest groups for the lack of civility in politics. And they demand we do better. At the same time, the very same voters who say they want political leaders to compromise and find common ground also say they are tired of leaders who compromise on their values and want them to stand up and fight the other side. Voters are sending mixed signals, and the result is messy.

The problem has come down to a matter of respect. Americans have stopped respecting our institutions, our political opponents, and even one another. That lack of respect has fueled a toxic polarization that has made this one of the most divided eras in modern history.

But there is hope. Having worked with Georgetown students over the past several years, Ed, Celinda, and I have seen that the next generation is willing and eager to take a different path. They are no less passionate about their politics, but they take a different approach. They listen to one another better. They challenge one another better. They find common ground better. When they don't, they agree to disagree better. In short, they respect one another better. And in listening to and working with them, they've made me better.

In this book, Ed and Celinda draw on their decades of friendship and collaboration to help us all understand how things got so bad while providing a blueprint for how we can turn things around. They don't agree on everything—not even in this book. But one thing they are *both* certain of is that it all comes down to a question of respect.

—**Mo Elleithee,**
Georgetown University,
Executive Director of the Institute of Politics & Public Service

Introduction

by Ed Goeas

At the height of the fall election in 2018, I had the opportunity to do a fellowship at Georgetown University's Institute of Politics and Public Service and built the discussions around the issue of civility in politics. It was halfway through President Trump's first term, an increasingly contentious political environment, and suburban women were moving away from the Republican Party in droves, driven by Donald Trump's tactless, disrespectful, and uncivil persona. It was a tough subject at a tough time. Every discussion had the potential of being pulled into the death spiral of incivility I felt our nation was in.

Throughout the three months of the fellowship at Georgetown, I was allowed to invite three outside guests to participate in one of the week's group discussions. In my fellowship on civility in politics, I asked three people I had come to highly respect during the forty-plus years I had worked on political campaigns. First was Ed Rollins, who I had been close friends with back when he was the political director at the White House for Ronald Reagan, and I

1

was the political director at the Republican National Congressional Committee. I wanted Rollins to share the story with the students about the final weeks of Reagan's re-election campaign in 1984, where he was the campaign manager. Rollins was trying to get President Reagan to go into Minnesota in the campaign's final days on the premise that Reagan would win the state if he did. Reagan's response: "It's Mondale's home state. Let him win it!"

And that is precisely what happened: Walter Mondale won Minnesota, with Reagan winning the other forty-nine states. I always saw that as a genuine act of civility, one that I doubt we would see in today's political environment and one that led to a very fascinating and positive discussion with the students. A discussion about showing respect for your political opponent and the fact that the 1984 campaign was the last presidential campaign void of negative political commercials on the airwaves.

The second person I brought in for a discussion group was Celinda Lake, the well-known Democratic pollster that I had conducted the Battleground Poll with for well over thirty years. I had come to respect Celinda over those years and had long considered her a good friend. Most of all, I had come to trust Celinda to be honest in her assessments of the data, both good and bad. I did not have Celinda join us to talk about polling; I brought her in to talk about campaign finance reform, an issue we talk about later in the book. I wanted her to be part of that discussion because we disagreed on the subject. We have very different answers to the needed campaign finance reform. Still, I liked having the students see a civil, respectful dialogue from polar viewpoints.

The third person I brought in for the last discussion group was Tom Ridge, ex-congressman, ex-governor of Pennsylvania, and the first secretary of Homeland Security. The governor had never been one of my polling clients, but I had known Tom Ridge from his first term in Congress and had always believed him to be one of the good guys who were there to make a difference, not cause trouble. I wanted him to talk with the students about Donald Trump. This discussion group was held ten days after the 2018 November Election, and we had just lost control of the US House of Representatives. There was a lot of post-election finger-pointing on the Republican side and vitriol on the Democratic side throughout Washington and the media. There were a lot of emotional comments about President Trump, and I wanted the students to see what the governor had to say. He made it clear that he would not defend the often-uncivil style Trump had become known for, but he said he "wished the best success for the president because if the president was successful, the country was successful."

I wanted the students to see what a true patriot was like. Tom Ridge had seen war in Vietnam, and he had put together a vast government agency to fight the war on terrorism. He knew when to fight and when to unite, and he was undoubtedly the perfect ending to our three-month discussion about civility.

As my fellowship ended, I must say, it was not the speakers but the students who inspired me to write this book. I found Georgetown University students somewhat different from many of the other students I have met while speaking on various campuses over the years. They were deeply committed to listening to different views with respect. I fed off the call for more from the five students assigned to me as a Student Strategy Team, whose assignment was to help facilitate the discussion groups. I saw in those students hope that we, as a nation, could pull out of this death spiral of incivility and realized the youth may very well be the key to building a better, more civil America.

I had also concluded, however, that the place for such a book would only come when Donald Trump was no longer president. I had always been outspoken about how I felt about his brash, tasteless style. I could never feel comfortable with the often stated, "I don't like his style, but I do like his policies." Not with two young sons at home who I was trying to teach to be everything Trump was not.

The bottom line was, I did not want the book to be Trump-centric, and I saw Trump as a symptom of where our country had devolved in our uncivil behaviors and not the actual disease. So when November came and Trump lost the presidency, I thought again about writing a book, but this time, with a slightly different idea—bring in Celinda Lake as a co-author. In 2019, we moved the Battleground Poll to Georgetown University and added a section about civility. It became the Georgetown Institute of Politics and Public Service Battleground Poll, but through 2019 and the election of 2020, the civility questions and analyses seemed to pique the reporters' interest in stories. Celinda and I agreed it was time to write and decided the book should not be Trump-centric.

Not be Trump-centric? That's been the most challenging part about writing this book and one that only you, the reader, can pass final judgment on. It was difficult not to join the chorus as I watched my party lose two Senate seats in Georgia and control of the United States Senate because all President Trump wanted to talk about was voter fraud and how voters' votes did not count, dampening Republican voter turnout in the Georgia runoff special election. It was hard to watch Donald Trump continue to trash Vice President Mike Pence, a man I had come to respect through the years, long before he was vice president, for not overturning the election with actions every intelligent legal mind in the country believed to be unconstitutional. It's been tough not to weave in the concern that over sixty percent of Republicans, nearly a quarter of the American electorate, believe Trump's unsubstantiated claims that the election was stolen. It's been hard not to be Trump-centric when he is so egocentric!

By Christmas of 2020, we had an agreement to write the book and do a Georgetown Institute of Politics and Public Service Battleground Poll the first week of January. Yes, we were in the field the week of January 6, with half the survey conducted before the events of that day and half conducted after. The data we received was beneficial in seeing the shifts in voter attitudes about civility because of the events of January 6.

Again, over the last year, part of me has often questioned writing this book, especially under the long, dark shadow cast by the events of January 6. I've had to deal with deeply held personal feelings. On 9/11 *and* January 6, my wife Lisa was there in the Senate office buildings, potentially in danger, as terrorists attacked our country—on 9/11, foreign terrorists, and on January 6, domestic terrorists. However, I keep coming back to the hope and inspiration I found in the students at Georgetown, the hope I see in my children, and the hope I see in my wife, working hard every day with her senator, Joni Ernst of Iowa, to try to make a positive difference in people's lives.

Over the last year, I realized something else working closely with Celinda to write this book. We were not writing a book on *civility*; we were writing about *respect*. Civility is how we language our communication. Respect is the essential core that informs how we interact with one another in all areas of life. Without respect, on a political or personal level, there is no possibility of coming together in meaningful, positive, healing ways—which we and the country desperately need. With that understanding, the demands for a public discussion about civility and respect seemed that much more significant, and the long dark shadows of January 6 seemed to be in retreat. Still, we are far from out of the woods. That's why I wrote this book with Celinda—crossing aisles and ideologies while agreeing about what needs to be done but often disagreeing on the practical solutions. We intend to model what's possible, even when people disagree.

I hope that what you are about to read will make a difference. Thank you for taking this journey with us.

Part One
The Great Divide

Chapter 1

Vanishing Respect: The Loss of Trust in an Uncivil Society

R ight now, this second, some place in America, someone is posting an uncivil tweet on Twitter. Right now,
someone on cable news is stoking anger within their
audience. Someone is disseminating misinformation online.
Someone is giving extreme voices a platform to sow discord and
dissension in our political arena. But also, right now, some place
in America, there *are* people respectfully working together to
strengthen our democracy.

Still, there is an urgent need to search for civility and unity in
our public discourse. We simply can't get much of anything done to
solve our core problems if we don't begin to come together. These
are not about ideological issues; they are about common sense and
human needs.

We Americans have an urgent decision facing us. We must
decide whether to build upon a foundation of mutual respect or
live in a fractured society, where division rules the day. Will we

work together for the common good by negotiating our differences in good faith or let our nation collapse? Will we guide each other toward a civil society in which our commonalities are acknowledged and celebrated, our differences respected, and where necessary, compromises can be agreeably negotiated?

We hope so. But for that to happen, respect and civility must return to American life and politics for our country to move forward. We like to think that, down deep, most Americans believe that too. Civil discourse means we make an effort to communicate effectively—and with kindness and consideration—even when we seem to be speaking different languages. Civility is the language of respect. Respect is the foundation of civil society, and the underlying foundation for respect is trust. Sadly, we no longer trust each other or our institutions.

Why have we allowed today's prevailing "us vs. them" mentality to take over? How have we lost our trust and regard for our fellow human beings' feelings and traditions? The lack of respect and trust, which we see in politics, social media, cable news shows, and in our personal lives, indicates a severe breakdown in the necessary components of a healthy democracy.

One would expect two pollsters—a Democrat and a Republican—to hold disparate opinions on many political and social issues. And we do. We also have areas of complete agreement. In our work and in writing this book together, our fundamental commitment is to help fix America's broken political system. This book explores where our country has gone wrong and offers solutions we both together and separately believe can lead us out of this mess.

Ed is a Republican, and Celinda is a Democrat. Interestingly, Ed grew up in a Democratic household and changed parties while in college. Celinda grew up in the Republican Party and likewise changed her party affiliation in college. This is not unique since many young adults transition from their parents' political parties. But having experiences in both parties has helped us understand the opposing beliefs more.

Over the years, we have done about a hundred surveys together for various groups, organizations, and causes. Our most significant collaboration is our Battleground Poll. This poll is a national bipartisan survey that reliably measures political opinion among voters in the United States. We've conducted this poll often over the past thirty years, the last four years, in partnership with Georgetown University's Institute of Politics and Public Service under the guidance of our close associate and friend, Mo Elleithee. Mo is currently the executive director of the Institute and the impetus behind making civility the focus on many of our Battleground topics and his ongoing Georgetown political programs.

Our Battleground Polls, which are conducted from our two different vantage points, seek to take the pulse of the American people. They are designed to help all intended parties and stakeholders—political leaders and aspiring leaders, media, and, most especially, the public-at-large—better understand their fellow Americans' feelings, attitudes, concerns, and fears.

A Foundation of Respect

Given our political differences, people often ask us how we met. It was the fall of 1990. Hungary had just withdrawn from the Warsaw Pact, but there were still Russian troops around that would not return to Moscow for another nine months. We were in Budapest at the request of the National Democratic Institute, both there separately, simply as observers to witness the country's first-ever free election. The streets, hotels, and government buildings were full of politicians, reporters, and assorted opportunists. Ghosts of the crushed 1956 uprising still roamed the ornate halls of the neo-Gothic Hungarian Parliament Building on the eastern banks of the Danube.

You often meet interesting individuals in a piano bar—where we first encountered one another. Budapest is composed of two cities, Buda and Pest. That night, we were on the Pest side, where a group of us had gathered at a hotel piano bar. After being introduced, we discovered we were both pollsters and talked long into the night about polling and politics. The idea for the Battleground Poll was conceived in Hungary. The streets we walked after that first meeting had been a battleground where the principles of freedom and democracy conquered the forces of tyranny. More than twenty-five hundred people gave their lives to throw off the yoke of oppression and create a representative democracy with free and open elections. Celinda remarked that this setting we were in was particularly poignant to her because her college roommate and best friend's family had fled from Hungary in 1956 for freedom after her friend's father, who was in the army, had given arms to the rebels.

That night, we decided to conduct a joint poll. The idea was simple: we would write a separate strategic analysis for the same polling data from Ed's Republican and Celinda's Democratic viewpoints. We would not see each other's strategic analysis until the evening before releasing it at a press conference. We also held the Republican and Democratic strategic analysis as "Veto Proof," so there was no watering down of either analysis. What made the Battleground Poll unique was telling both sides of the story from a singularly focused perspective. Our first joint poll came out nine months after our first meeting—in June 1991—and ended up being the first publicly released poll showing potential problems for President H.W. Bush's re-election in 1992.

Over time, we developed a second component to the Battleground Poll, the Civility Poll. Its purpose was to measure and track voter attitudes on civility in our politics and public spaces. The Georgetown Institute of Politics and Public Service Civility Poll gathers and analyzes voters' opinions and shows how Americans have viewed the question of compromise and finding common ground in politics at various points in time.

In our latest polls, we have uncovered evidence of a widening gap in the American population that potentially threatens the very foundations of our democracy. We have discovered that almost every group of Americans feels victimized somehow. Some strongly believe in the power of a free market and resent government intervention and restrictions in every facet of their daily lives. Others believe in far more government involvement to give everyone a fair chance and protect them against special interests and the privileged few.

The noise level has risen from both arenas, and we are rapidly losing the ability to even hear each other. With too few of us listening, and in-person interactions dramatically diminished, polarization will continue to escalate, with dissension center stage in the media, in our city and country streets and public gathering places, and even at our family dining tables.

In our Battleground Polls, we see a confusing contradiction again and again. The vast majority of the people we polled say they want cooperation. They *say* they want us to forge mutual respect. They *say* they will elect politicians willing to compromise for the greater good. At the same time, these respondents are unwilling to "give in" to compromise on many issues that separate them. Fortunately, they agree on many topics, such as the need to fix our crumbling infrastructure, shore up our coastlines, fight wildfires, make prescription drugs affordable, and help small businesses. Still, fighting continues about how much taxpayer money to allocate and how to implement these goals.

In truth, politicians walk a thin line. Voters want the politicians they've elected to stand up for what their constituents believe in but come together as well. So finding ways to compromise effectively and not alienate your base is not easy for even the most skillful elected official.

The hard truth is that without mutual respect, there can be no common ground. Without it, this yawning chasm between us will continue to widen until it not only stalls critical issues but threatens to erupt into the kind of violence we saw on the January 6, 2021, attack in the Capitol—or worse.

Our Democratic Republic has a Constitution and Bill of Rights that guarantee each American the right to life, liberty, and the pursuit of happiness. We love to call ourselves a melting pot or a "mosaic," where everyone retains their differences but combines them into a beautiful whole. Yet on closer look, the reality of America is that it has rarely been a place of complete unity and serenity. Democracies and republics tend to be messy. They require the accommodation of competing ideas and interests. Minor rebellions, assassinations, social unrest, violence, civil war, and pandemics have all occurred in American history. Some old-timers and even Baby Boomers like to argue that things have been worse in years past, and they all eventually got better. The bottom line is not about which generation had the most significant challenges. We see things getting worse for us now and want to fix those areas.

Today, there are fewer areas where people agree, making it much harder to get things done. In President Biden's inaugural speech, he called for restoring a sense of unity.[2] That *is* highly desirable, but is it attainable? We can't seem to agree on what it even means to *be unified*. This is why we structure our Battleground Polls to ask questions carefully, ensuring responders will provide honest feedback on how they perceive things on the deep divide. Of course, the biggest question, the most difficult to answer, and what we're exploring here is, *"What can we do about it?"*

Finding solutions is more complicated than ever. Technology is connecting us at astounding rates, but social media is a blessing *and* a curse. With everyone having a voice and hiding behind anonymity, it is both isolating and polarizing in unique ways. For instance, online algorithms are specifically designed to reinforce what we already like. We're sure you've experienced this—we have! You go shopping on Amazon, and suddenly, you see ads for similar things, or even the very same thing, following you on to every website you visit. That is also true in politics. Algorithms will recognize that you clicked on Donald Trump's website or some related feed. This means you must like Trump, be aligned with Republicans, or have Conservative ideas—and everything on your social media feed will be pro-Trump or in that vein.

Thanks to our upbringing, despite some sharp contrasts, we also have many areas of common ground. We both view our polling work as a public service, bringing the voice of the people to our democracy. We are equally determined to make life better for others. We each came from rural states rather than urban centers and families that stressed cooperation. Both sets of parents instilled in us the need for active citizen participation. We are also both people of faith. As said earlier, that we each started in a different political party gave us a greater understanding of those who think differently—and with that knowledge comes tolerance.

Ed's Background

I was born in San Francisco right after my father graduated college, entered his chosen career with the US Army, and moved to Fort Bliss, Texas, six weeks later. This was the first of many assignments throughout his long and distinguished career in the Armed Forces. We frequently moved and lived in multiple states and abroad throughout my childhood. My father did tours in Vietnam, Korea, and, at the tail end of his career, in Germany. I graduated from high school there in 1970, after I attended fifteen schools between kindergarten and college, including schools in Texas, Washington, California, Maryland, Oklahoma, and Kansas. Our family vacations were often car trips across the US between new assignments. I didn't realize it at the time, but this exposure was a positive life experience, opening me up to the world to see how different people live. My father eventually retired, earning the rank of Lt. Colonel. I proudly wore the label of "Army Brat."

My father was born in Hawaii and was of Portuguese descent. Because our family years were dotted with many temporary homes, he especially emphasized our family's Portuguese heritage and Hawaiian culture. In the early days of Hawaii, Portuguese immigrants were by far the minority, often working as field workers or merchants. In contrast, my mother was from a small town in the mountains of Tennessee. Her parents were brought up in those mountains. Still, during the Great Depression, when she was an infant, her parents left her with her grandmother and went in different directions to find jobs elsewhere and never returned, never came back together as a family.

My dad's family had been in Hawaii for over sixty years when the attack on Pearl Harbor happened. My father was walking home from serving Mass as an altar boy that Sunday morning when he saw the smoke filling the horizon. That horrific event not only brought our country together and Hawaiians themselves together, but it also drove my father's commitment to public service and military service at a very young age. It also instilled in him a strong dislike for bullies and a commitment to stand up for the "Little Guy." These are qualities I like to think he passed on to me and that I can pass on to my children.

The coming together of Hawaii also had another impact on my extended family and my view of the world. I have gained cousins of mixed Samoan and Hawaiian heritage through the years, with perhaps a few other ethnicities thrown in. They may not be familiar with their Portuguese heritage, but we share our Hawaiian culture. To me, the melting pot or mosaic—whatever you care to call it—is what's unique about this country, which offers the promise of a better life for everyone willing to work both hard and together.

A speech impediment made me a quieter adolescent than most; in retrospect, I consider that a blessing in disguise that helped me become a good listener. I found that if you keep your mouth closed and ears open and focus on the task at hand, you can have access to environments where you hear and see a lot.

I also learned from my father the importance of ethical decisions. Not that I've always made the right decisions, but it has certainly kept me from making more than my share of bad choices. While my father encouraged my involvement in politics from a public service standpoint, he was a firm believer in the phrase, "Power corrupts, and absolute power corrupts absolutely!" He often advised me that "if you have to question the ethical right and wrong of something you are faced with, you already have your answer."

My involvement in politics started in 1964, at age twelve, while my father was in Vietnam, and I volunteered at the local headquarters of the Lyndon Johnson presidential campaign, wanting to understand why my father was there and not home with us. And, as a Catholic, I believed I had to be with the party of John Kennedy. I was essentially "licking envelopes" while soaking up the excitement of Johnson's campaign against Barry Goldwater but was "adopted" by several college girls working in the campaign—being the kid whose father was in Vietnam. I learned a lot, but most of all ended that campaign and became increasingly interested in politics.

In 1970, I attended Cameron University in Lawton, Oklahoma. In 1972, while in college, I volunteered on campus for George McGovern in his campaign against Richard Nixon. It was a campaign primarily driven by the student movement, and I was bothered when, after McGovern won the nomination, the unions backed McGovern. Suddenly, the students were all but dismissed. They essentially just patted us on the head and said, "Nice little college students. We will take over now. Let the adults work." It was the first crack in my staunch Democratic identification.

I was also involved in a statewide student group called the Oklahoma Intercollegiate Legislature (OIL) through those college years, modeled after the actual State Legislature. It was established to bring the student movement off the streets and into a format where our voices would be heard from inside the structure, with events like the 1970 killing of five protesting students killed by the Ohio National Guard at Kent State University in Ohio serving as a significant catalyst. In my junior and senior years, I was elected a "governor," running my first populist campaign by unifying the smaller universities versus the larger state schools. My activism caught the attention of Frank Keating, a twenty-five-year-old Republican state senator from Oklahoma. Frank was up for reelection and actively looking for student leaders. He contacted me and asked me to become a Republican and part of his campaign. While, by that time, I was increasingly identifying with Republican ideas—of the more centrist persuasion—I told him I could not belong to the same party as Nixon. One year later, Keating, then running for Congress, called again. "Nixon is out. No more excuses," he said. "Come work with us." I left college just seven credits short of graduation to run Keating's campaign—my first paid political position. Although Keating lost that election, he would eventually become a two-term governor of Oklahoma, with me helping at times, as we had forged a solid and enduring friendship.

I spent the next decade working in various positions at the Republican National Committee and the National Republican Congressional Committee and even a two-year stint as chief of staff for a congressman from Indiana. During that time, I met Republican pollster Lance Tarrance, and in 1987, joined his firm to open a Washington office for Tarrance and Associates. One year later, Tarrance decided to sell this firm to Gallup and step back from politics, and I was fortunate to be moved up to become the firm's president. In 1991, I, along with my two partners, Brian Tringali and Dave Sackett, bought the Tarrance Group from Gallup. We have worked together, running it as partners, ever since.

In those thirty-plus years as a pollster and through many campaigns as part of the strategy teams, I have seen political campaigns and political dialogue become increasingly hostile. I have also seen trust in government and institutions turn cynical. Some of that distrust is driven by our falling into the trap of dealing with all problems from a position of ideology—when not all solutions have anything to do with ideology. Much of that distrust is driven by a lack of solutions to problems people face every day. I have repeatedly watched our nation go through problem-solving phases where we talk about the issue, talk about solutions, implement solutions, and then create a new set of problems. We have gone through those phases so many times that the new problems we must deal with are problems created by our solutions and not the root problems. The voters sense their root problems are not being addressed, making them more cynical. Lacking trust makes them more susceptible to demagoguery, whether from candidates, special interest groups, social media, or the news media.

One of the first times I addressed this issue in a meaningful way was during the eight-session fellowship I did at Georgetown University's Institute of Politics and Public Service in 2018. Thanks to my enlightening conversations with the Georgetown University students, this fellowship became the catalyst for this book.

Celinda's Background

I grew up in Montana on a cattle ranch between Livingston and Bozeman. My family was kind of old-school moderates, more of a libertarian sort of Republican than many of their neighbors, consistently pro-choice, conservationists, and always available to those in need. My parents moved from New York City to Montana after World War II. After being in the infantry in Normandy and the Battle of the Bulge, my dad thought, "How tough could going out West be?" My mom, who has never been west of Pennsylvania, was independent and up for an adventure. In 1948, they bought a ranch in Montana but didn't have enough money for cattle—a tough way to make a living. My dad learned ranching while trying to help other people save their herds in the awful winter of '48. In ranch culture, there were, and I believe still are, two powerful ethical principles that revolved around respect and trust in each other.

The first was that you minded your own business. People didn't interfere. There's a real libertarian streak in Montana about not judging other people. The other was helping people out, especially when something terrible happened. When I was pretty young, my dad broke his leg feeding cattle, and many people came to his aid.

When a terrible snowstorm hit the town or a fire burned down a barn, people would be there the following day. There were no questions asked and no judgments about what you believed; they just came to pitch in and help rebuild. People brought food to each other if someone in the family was sick or after a birth or death. There was just an authentic culture of pitching in and helping out.

We shared a fence line with our newest neighbors, and we would always do joint fence repairs. We would set aside a date for both families to work along the fence line and repair it. When I was little, I thought we didn't like one of our neighbors that well. My dad said at breakfast, "Today, we all have to fix the fence together."

I told him, "I thought we didn't like those neighbors."

My dad said to me, "First of all, do not ever say that. That is not appropriate. Second, liking them has nothing to do with that. We work together to protect our fence line for each of our herds of cattle, and we're always going to be polite and respectful. You're always going to call our neighbors Mr. and Mrs."

There was a very deep-seated sense that you had a shared stake in everyone's success. That you could work together, even if you disagreed on some points of view. There needs to be more of this sense of looking out for each other, of helping each other "mend fences," especially in times of need.

My parents firmly believed in good public schools, even though they had gone to private schools. They drove us across county lines every day to the town they thought had the best schools. Early on, they taught us to have our own opinions. They would each pick a different candidate in the Republican Primary, and we would have to form our own opinions and respect people with different views.

I became a pollster because I had always liked politics and was a member of Teenage Republicans and an officeholder in the organization. I chose a women's college because I had faced closed doors as a girl in high school. I had wanted to be student body president but was told I needed to run for secretary instead, which I won. I beat the boys and the girls on the speech team, and people shunned rather than celebrated my success. I decided I was going to a school that made and supported women leaders. In 1971, when I started at Smith College, the Women's Movement and the Vietnam War were raging. The Women's Movement had some Republican support. My first introduction to real polarization was the fight between the Democrats and attorney Phyllis Schlafly, who campaigned against adding the Equal Rights Amendment to the US Constitution.

The Vietnam War was also a factor in my changing parties. I had gone to high school where half of the people didn't go to college, which meant that many were called up to serve in Vietnam. On the first day at my college, we held a demonstration where we went to the airport near the college to protest against the Vietnam War. Many students from the East Coast were shouting at the young recruits. They were like the kids I had gone to high school with. Most of them did not want to go to Vietnam. Those sets of contradictions were, in large part, what made me a Democrat. I was also influenced by consumer rights, corporate accountability, the Public Interest Research Group, and other citizen movements that Ralph Nader was starting, all widely popular on college campuses. Grassroots-oriented politics, the idea of taking the voices of the people to Washington, appealed to me.

Abroad in Geneva for my junior year, I decided to go to law school to become a US Equal Employment Opportunity Commission lawyer. However, in Geneva, I met some expatriate Americans who had studied international voting behavior at the University of Michigan. As part of their studies, they researched American voting behavior and surveys. I was utterly captivated by what they discussed and changed majors from pre-law to American political behavior. At the University of Michigan, I worked on the National Election Studies, dedicated to bringing the voices of our voters to the table.

While in graduate school at the University of Michigan, I decided to leave every two years to participate in politics. In 1982, I finished my master's degree on the gender gap and then wrote a pre-dissertation study on the differences between men's and women's candidate campaigns. My passion for progressive politics and women in politics was cemented.

Instead of completing my PhD, I decided to be directly involved in politics. I went to Washington, DC, to work on Walter Mondale and Geraldine Ferraro's 1984 presidential campaign with highly respected pollster Peter Hart. I went on the Hill to work for Pat Williams, my Montana congressman. Both he and his wife, Carol Williams, strongly supported women's leadership. Then I went to work for a bipartisan pro-choice PAC, The Women's Campaign Fund. In 1989, I joined pollster Stan Greenberg in his firm. In 1995, I started my company, Lake Research Partners with a fellow woman partner—Alysia Snell. I wanted to have a firm committed to change, built on the needs and objectives of women candidates, women voters, and people of color. I wanted to head up a progressive firm.

A central theme of this book for both of us is that you can't have respect if you don't start with trust, and you can't have that trust when people don't appreciate each other's everyday experiences. This partnership between the pollster son of a Democratic family and the pollster daughter of a Republican family is not accidental. Interestingly, I have many friends in my network who say they don't know a Republican, never met one in their life, and generally don't trust them. If I distrusted all Republicans, I would have to start with my mother and my dad, the people I loved most in the world.

Where We Are and Can Go

Over the past thirty years, our clients have included presidential candidates and sitting presidents, governors, hundreds of congressional and legislative leaders, and change-making leaders of every stripe. We're proud of the prestigious "Distinguished Service Award," which the American Association of Political Consultants honored us with in 2016 for our Battleground Polls.

In addition to our professional experience and work, we are also fellow American citizens, part of a community, a family, and our circles of friends. In each of these roles, we see why the current climate of incivility is ill-serving all of us. In recent Battleground Polls, we've seen voters increasingly rank "division in the country" among the most critical issues facing them personally, even while becoming increasingly polarized over the country's direction and many vital matters.

It was no surprise that all voters rank political polarization among their top concerns. These polarizing numbers mean it will be increasingly difficult to address the problems we face as a nation until we find a way to compromise and stand together on a firm middle ground. To make sure we are headed in the right direction, we *all* need to take responsibility. It's easy to have an opinion and express it, but we need to do more than continue to complain about each other.

We are all citizens of this country we share, and along with our guaranteed rights come responsibilities. We must all take part in rebuilding a civil society based on mutual respect. Our voices carry weight in our families, workplaces, and communities. In how we conduct ourselves daily, we can serve as models of civility. We can influence the character of our political dialogue with our words, our actions, our pocketbooks—and our votes.

With so many disturbing factors working against us, is a new age of civility and respect even *possible*? Even though it won't be easy, we believe *it is* possible. Supreme Court Justices Antonin Scalia and Ruth Bader Ginsburg were profoundly respectful and close in an unlikely friendship between the two most influential justices at opposite ends of the political spectrum. Similarly, John McCain and Joe Biden had a warm and respectful personal and professional relationship despite their ideological differences on many issues. In Joe Biden's eulogy at John McCain's memorial service on August 30, 2018, in the Washington National Cathedral, he said, in part: "John loved basic values, fairness, honesty, dignity, respect, giving hate no safe harbor, leaving no one behind, and understanding Americans were part of something much bigger than ourselves."[3]

There will constantly be changing circumstances and challenges ahead. Still, despite this heated era, we must not lose the fundamentals. We Americans must look out for each other's best interests—for, as we will show you, our individual best interests are in the collective best interests of our beloved nation as a whole.

Chapter 2

Cynicism: Many Americans Doubt There *Are* Solutions

N ow that we have examined one of the root causes of polarization among Americans, we need to understand why we as a nation have become extremely cynical. Make no mistake; a deep vein of cynicism runs through the fabric of American society. We are turning against each other in new and dangerous ways. We look at each other with mistrust. Many of us no longer talk to our neighbors. We no longer have faith in the institutions—the churches, universities, and centers of government, among other public entities—that have been the bedrock of our commonality for so long.

We have become strangers to one another, as mistrust replaces respect at every turn. Given the corrosive nature of cynicism, before moving forward is possible, we need to understand what elements and factors make it so destructive.

Portraying a large segment of the American public as cynical may seem cynical, but data reinforces this phenomenon. The

American National Election Studies (ANES) agency, whose mission is "to provide researchers with a view of the political world through the eyes of ordinary citizens," is a collaboration between Stanford University and the University of Michigan, with funding from the National Science Foundation. This group regularly conducts a Trust in Government Survey. They have a "trust score" metric that goes up to a maximum trust level of 50. This score peaked at 47 during the height of the Reagan presidency. In 2016, it plummeted to an all-time low of 17. And in 2019, a Pew Research poll found that only 42 percent of Americans feel confident that civil conversations are possible between people who hold opposing views.[4]

What is driving American voters into a cynical mindset? First, it's important to point out that cynical voters are not monotheistic, or one size fits all. What they have in common is their deep frustration, feeling that their real-life problems are not being met. Many Americans doubt solutions are coming from *any* institutions, that no one is looking out for them, except for the two entities they still trust—firefighters and the military.

We posit that three main factors drive American voters into a cynical mindset. *First*: Essentially, voters are cynical because their needs are not being met. *Second*: Many Americans feel that our most elite institutions are corrupt and fail us when we need them most. *Third*: Political solutions often create new problems when trying to fix old ones. Put all three together, and you've got a toxic situation that rewards the worst aspects of our society.

One goal of this book is to offer ways to awaken the "better angels" of our nature to decrease cynicism and increase trust between Americans and our institutions. We don't claim to have all the answers. Still, we hope to present some solutions that can help reposition America as a place where one can trust their neighbor, raise children safely, and live freely and respectfully within a nation of differences.

The Threat Cynicism Poses

Cynicism is a problem that has many levels. For one thing, a cynical voter is the most easily manipulated by demagoguery. Unfortunately, some politicians and media skillfully use this rampant cynicism to influence and divide us. Candidates manipulate voters by sometimes exaggerating merely theoretical threats from outside groups. Not trusting each other makes us much more prepared to assault each other. Frustration often turns to anger, which fuels cynicism. Demagogues feed off that negativity. It was cynical voters who largely facilitated the presidential election of Donald Trump. The most common phrase we heard in support of Trump was "he speaks for us," especially in rural America. He often did not; he just tapped into voters' anger and frustration, then turned up the volume on that anger and frustration. The campaign was usually void of solutions, but many cynical voters thought he did speak for them, and that was all that mattered in getting their vote.

Humans are social creatures who form networks and affinity groups. Over time, such collective groups often facilitate trends toward conformity and extremism. Members of a group are far more likely to share information with those members who support their beliefs. The lack of diversity in thinking and dialogue results in a movement away from each other—and that is where civil dialogue and compromise can occur. The ensuing lack of engagement leads to increased suspicion and hostility toward opposing groups.

Ed Analyzes the Illusive Process of Root Problem-Solving

I've always liked to think of myself as an optimist. I chose to be an optimist, which is not always an easy route in today's political environment. When I'm in a situation where a contentious issue is being discussed, I often try to diffuse the situation by recognizing the merits of both sides. As an optimist, it hurts to see how cynicism is tearing apart the kind of life we Americans have worked so hard to create. In a recent Battleground Poll, we found that a distressing number of our fellow citizens (87 percent) are very concerned about the ability of our leaders to solve our most significant issues.

Most elected officials in today's political environment do not understand why the cycle of the four steps of problem-solving has contributed so heavily to today's cynical voter development. Here's the repetitive loop of the four stages of problem-solving: 1) We talk about the problem, 2) we talk about solutions, 3) we implement solutions, and 4) those solutions create new problems. Unfortunately, we as a nation have been through that cycle so many times that, more often than not, we are dealing with problems created by our solutions and not the root problems the American public faces every day! When voters see these problems remain, year after year, campaign after campaign, their cynicism only grows deeper.

It is interesting to look back at how our forefathers saw this inherent problem when discussing solutions. As the story goes, in a conversation between Thomas Jefferson and George Washington, upon Jefferson's return from France after being gone during the Constitutional Convention, they were having tea when Jefferson asked why they had created the Senate and the House. Washington asked Jefferson why he poured his hot tea into his saucer before drinking it. When Jefferson responded, "To let it cool," Washington supposedly answered. That was why they created the Senate: to pour our legislation into the Senate and let it cool. Our forefathers understood we needed to pause in that third phase of problem-solving to ensure we were not creating more significant problems than those we were trying to solve.

I could give dozens of examples about our going through this cycle of problem-solving throughout history. Before I do, let me first explain how I have learned to share the data from our surveys at The Tarrance Group. Every survey is not just a set of numbers; the numbers tell a story. What are the candidate's strengths and weaknesses? What are the issues most directly affecting the daily lives of the voters? How are solutions accepted or rejected by the voters, both pro and con? The story of those combined numbers paints the picture of the campaign's strategy.

I believe one of the reasons for telling the story behind the numbers comes naturally from something my father taught me about the Hawaiian culture called "Talk Story," as we moved from state to state and even abroad. When you Talk Story in Hawaii, it is much more personal. It can be several anecdotes tied to a lesson or just a funny ending. It's a fantastic concept because it makes you stop and consider the person in front of you as a living human being with desires, hopes, dreams, successes, and failures. It makes you relate to people as whole individuals. When you do that with survey numbers, it brings those numbers alive and helps the candidate and campaign connect better to the voters they seek to represent. It is certainly something we need more of in today's political environment.

But again, I could give dozens of examples about our going through this cycle of problem-solving throughout history. In recent years, one of the best examples is "Obamacare," officially known as the "Affordable Care Act." When I say recent years, perhaps I should say over more than a decade because Obamacare was signed into law in March 2010, and Republicans and Democrats have been fighting over it ever since.

The Affordable Care Act had three main goals, according to Healthcare.gov: to "make affordable health insurance available to more people," "expand the Medicaid program," and "support innovative medical care delivery methods designed to lower the costs of healthcare."[5] Where Obamacare fell short over the last decade is in the area of costs. While Democrats and Republicans have been fighting in Washington over the legal existence of Obamacare, there was a basic premise of the legislation that was contradicted in the final passage. That premise was that males under the age of thirty-five would start participating in the healthcare system and bring more money into the system. What was found when looking at the system at that time was that many young males (especially white males) were not buying health insurance. After leaving home, they were not participants in the health system because they often did not see the need.

The premise was that pulling them in as participants of the healthcare system would help offset costs driven by senior adults. Unfortunately, two things were put into the legislation that undercut that basic premise. First, an amendment allowed children to stay on their parents' health insurance until they were twenty-seven years old. While well-meaning in intention, it undercuts the original premise of getting these young adults to contribute into the healthcare system. Second, penalties for not participating in the healthcare system were far less than the costs of participating, so many of these younger male voters continued to opt out and just paid the penalty.

From Ed's point of view, he notes, "Now, a decade later, our national campaigns continue to go back and forth on the issue. Democrats continue to be faced with the outcomes of over-promising, costs continue to be a problem for broad swaths of the American public, and many cannot "keep their doctor." Republicans continued to campaign against the system of Obamacare as a whole, both with the public and in the courts, rather than taking that third step of problem-solving, which is to slow it down and look for ways to make it better. Meanwhile, voters continued to grow more cynical about both the healthcare issue and Washington, DC in general, to the ability of our government to address problems in their daily lives.

Celinda Offers Data-Driven Analysis

Ed is a story-driven man; I'm a data-driven woman. Sometimes, when men come into a room with their ideas, I want to put my numbers right down on the table. So let me explain how I see this problem of voter cynicism in terms of numbers. A Pew Research-Public Trust in Government Survey from 1958 to 2021 showed that public trust in government has steadily eroded since the 1960s.[6] There have only been slight recoveries in the Reagan, Clinton, and Bush administrations when confidence in the government remained consistently low. The following graph, taken from The ANES Trust in Government Index this year (2022), illustrates this decline:

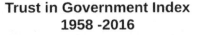

**Trust in Government Index
1958 -2016**

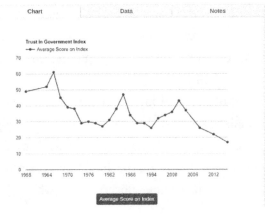

When Ed and I disagree, our policy arguments often begin with differences in how we feel about spending levels and the mechanics between the political parties, but not our shared values and goals. For me, the most promising sign of our moving back toward the center is the unity promoted by the new administration. In his inaugural address, Joe Biden said, "We can see each other not as adversaries but as neighbors. We can treat each other with dignity and respect."[7] Let's hope President Biden is right, that we *can* see each other as neighbors, not as adversaries, and appreciate each other's everyday experiences as fellow Americans.

Weaponizing Grievances

All political campaigns have two main objectives. The first is their need to mobilize likely supporters to get out and vote. Second, they need to persuade undecided people to vote for their candidates and their party's agendas. Mobilization means telling people why their vote is meaningful and why they should vote. It is easier to mobilize someone who is already likely to agree with you than to convince someone unsure. Today's big data has made mobilization more straightforward, affordable, and effective. In past years, campaign mobilizations mainly involved driving up to someone's house, knocking on their door, and urging them to vote. Technology has made this outreach far easier. Campaigns always have limited resources, so putting more money into mobilization gets them a bigger bang for their buck.

The amount of personal information political campaigns have about individuals is now off the charts. Politicians can paint a personal profile for every single registered voter. They can access a detailed and accurate profile of you based on how often you vote, your zip code, your magazine subscriptions, what television programs you watch, your social media habits, and your computer clicks. In the past, they could only do that at the neighborhood level. Now, it can be done at the individual household level. Given all this data about voters, it is easier for stakeholders to find those people.

Again, campaigns emphasize mobilization over persuasion since it takes fewer resources to get someone who agrees with you to engage. Donald Trump won in 2016 mainly because his campaign team went out and found "sleepy Republicans"—those who wouldn't usually vote but who fervently agreed with him. They weren't typical voters, but his team convinced them it was worth their time to go to the polls. Obama did the same thing in 2008. He found people who did not usually go out to vote but were predisposed to support him, and he brought them out to vote.

We are not saying that focusing mainly on mobilization is inherently the wrong way to get voters to participate in democracy. But cynicism and polarization can be enhanced if the equation is imbalanced toward mobilization, especially if campaigns feel they can win without speaking to the undecided voters instead of focusing on their base. Mobilizing can be an incredibly effective strategy for winning, but the chasms that separate Americans only deepen if candidates don't bring along anyone other than those who already agree with them.

Now, campaigns have started preaching mainly to the choir. That is why Marjorie Taylor Greene, who is seen by many as a terrible voice of division, was able to raise millions of dollars in a short period, even after being stripped of her committee assignments for promoting conspiracy theories and anti-Semitic remarks. It's also why Donald Trump shocked the world with his presidential victory. He didn't speak for most Americans, but he mobilized his base and was incredibly effective.

Mobilization based on divisive issues and feelings further decreases our faith in one another and weakens the strengths that make us Americans. How can we move forward with confidence in family, education, and our ability to better ourselves if we can't agree on the actual election results? Yet many Republicans remain skeptical about the 2020 presidential election results. A Reuters/Ipsos poll from April 2021 found that 55 percent of Republicans believe the presidential election was "unfair or rigged" and that 60 percent of Republicans think the election was "stolen" from Donald Trump. Traditionally, between 8 and 14 percent of voters always refuse to accept the legitimacy of presidential elections. That number has soared in the aftermath of the 2020 presidential election.[8]

The former president's refusal to accept his defeat is responsible for a considerable increase in the number of cynical voters that have lost faith in the election process. Social media and conservative news outlets have served to spread disinformation. The question going forward is the lasting impact on future voter turnout. Evidence is clear that all of the post-election noise about the election being stolen and Republican votes not being counted led to the defeat of the two incumbent Republican senators thrown into a special election runoff in Georgia after the November election. The constant drumbeat about the stolen presidential election and their vote not counting suppressed Republican turnout, allowing both Democratic senate candidates to squeak by their Republican opponents. Those defeats resulted in the Republicans losing control of the Senate.

Senator Mitt Romney has been one of the few Republican voices of reason and reconciliation. After the 2020 presidential election, he said, "Look, I lost in 2012. I have people today who say, 'Hey, you know what? You won.' But I didn't. I lost fair and square. Spreading this kind of rumor about our election system not working is dangerous for democracy here and abroad."[9]

Again, mass-scale misinformation systematically erodes public trust and turns groups against each other. An unemployed steelworker has more in common with a hardworking immigrant than either of them does with Donald Trump. Neither of them should be cynical about America because America can work for both when America has its ideals in place.

Gerrymandering Increases Cynicism

People need to know their vote counts to feel optimistic about the American electoral system. It does. Each voice has always mattered. But a process known as gerrymandering—manipulating political boundaries to produce votes for those doing the manipulation—has understandably made many feel disenfranchised. The contentious rhetoric surrounding the issue has done little to correct those feelings of disfranchisement.

Redistricting is an established and necessary aspect of democracy. Populations change over the years, so new congressional and state legislative district boundaries must be drawn. In some situations, this essential and warranted process to assure appropriate representation has been hijacked by gerrymandering that is being used politically by both Democrats and Republicans.

In the primaries, less than 20 percent of registered voters turn out, often concentrating power toward the ideological extremes of both parties and away from the center. In those primary elections, gerrymandering often favors extremist, ideological candidates over more centrist ones. In other words, candidates must pander to their constituency's more radical far-right and far-left elements or risk losing in the primary. It's important for candidates who are liberal or conservative to have to persuade voters who are more in the middle that they have the better solutions. With many state legislators drawing the gerrymandered voting districts into their party's strongholds, those primary candidates often became de facto winners of the general elections—only further driving voters' feelings of disfranchisement.

One look at any congressional map will tell you that we need to redraw boundaries to make primaries more competitive. In 2018, in North Carolina and Ohio, Democratic candidates earned 48 to 50 percent of the vote yet won only 25 percent of the seats in those states due to districts carved into Republican strongholds. (In North Carolina, for the 2020 election, courts forced the state to redistrict before the election, and that margin improved for the Democrats—receiving 48 percent of the votes and 38 percent of the congressional seats.) The knife cuts both ways; in Democratically-controlled Maryland, most of the turnover seats were in districts drawn by commissions and the courts instead of by bi-partisan state legislatures.

Republicans prefer to "pack" minority voters into predominantly Black or minority districts while keeping Republican districts distinct. Republicans began focusing on creating these minority districts with redistricting from the 1990 Census, often coordinating these efforts with the Black community. Republicans argued that with the Democrats spreading the Black vote across multiple districts to strengthen the Democrat vote in those districts, they were not getting their due representation in Congress. There is some merit to that point. Following the 1980 redistricting, there were only nineteen Black members of Congress. Today, following the 2020 election, there are fifty-nine Black members of Congress, which comprises 12.7 percent of the US House of Representatives and closely matches the 2020 Census, which has 12.4 percent of the country's population as Black.

Democrats argue that by Republicans compacting those minority votes, which results in their increasing their party's representatives, they effectively disenfranchised those Black voters. In court, North Carolina's redistricting maps were successfully challenged because they disenfranchised minority voters, and the Supreme Court upheld the lower court's decision.

Democrats aim to "crack" minority voters into different districts to give the Democratic Party an electoral advantage. Black voters in Maryland were unfairly targeted in gerrymandered maps because it would have created an additional Republican seat. Often, it is politically expedient to both "pack" or "crack" minorities. Either way, some argue this dilutes the political power of people of color.

Article 5 of the Civil Rights Act required states with a history of systemic racism to get federal approval for any redistricting plans. In 2003, the Supreme Court struck down Article 5 and opened a Pandora's Box of Jim Crow legislation and gerrymandering. Citizen groups and nonprofits that wish to challenge gerrymandered maps are routinely forced to incur legal costs in the millions of dollars. Delay tactics are also common; lawmakers use the delays to increase the cost of litigation as they shore up their political power base.

Another issue that impacts redistricting is known as "trifectas." The Trifecta phenomenon is where one party controls the governor's mansion, the state Senate, and the State House of Representatives/Assembly, which is to say that the party controls the entire political process. After the 2010 elections, Republicans picked up twelve new trifecta states for a total of twenty states, and the

Democrats lost five trifecta states, taking them down to only eleven states. The net result in those thirty-one states that comprised the trifecta states in the 2012 election was that the Democrats lost sixteen seats and the Republicans picked up 132 new seats. A party's trifecta status can be determinative in states where legislatures and governors dominate the redistricting process.

Gerrymandering reforms are needed that will outline stringent requirements for redrawing voting districts. Establishing independent commissions representing the states' ethnic makeup would draw boundaries that ensure minority representation and greater competition among candidates. Communities sharing common interests should remain together in the same district.

Seven in ten voters approve of using independent commissions to redraw district boundaries. Encouragingly, redistricting reform legislation was passed in 2018 and 2020 by large margins in many states. More needs to be done. We must increase transparency in the process of drawing electoral districts. Criteria would be standardized, and the commissions would be bipartisan. Maps drawn would be subject to oversight and review. The days of political backroom dealing need to end, and while it will take effort, we believe that must, can, and will happen.

The Path to Optimism

The American voter *is* cynical. Technology and campaigns do divide us. Many people feel their votes don't count and that our institutions fail us. Where *do* we go from here? Over the past several years, a range of organizations, spanning academia, faith, business, and civil society, have offered a wide variety of best practices, including meaningful dialogue with others and implementing positive change in local communities.

An example at the national level of cross-partisan groups coming together to defend and reform our democracy is the United America Network, launched in October 2021 in Austin, Texas. Over one hundred-plus philanthropists and leaders met at that first meeting and committed to working together to protect elections, win reforms, and build a positive movement to strengthen nonpartisan democracy defense and deal in a bipartisan way with contentious issues like election reform, gerrymandering, and reforms surrounding primaries.

The Massachusetts Institute of Technology (MIT) has developed its Local Voices Network (LVN) program at the local level. This online discussion platform amplifies unheard voices to encourage public understanding and promote better policy development. The LVN engages people in the community to share their diverse perspectives through a series of moderated and recorded discussions designed to advance understanding of often thorny issues. This constructive conversation model invites people to understand their roles and importance within complex social problems, hearing it from local voices—some with whom they disagree. Those who listen and learn can break out of the "echo chamber" of news programs and social media algorithms and interact comfortably with neighbors who hold competing views. This kind of humanization of political discourse can be a powerful tool in promoting civility.

There is tremendous power for good in actively listening and learning from other Americans, and one way to set norms of respectful discourse is to join local groups. We can all move forward in our everyday lives through positive actions, values, and contributions to our communities. A good example from Celinda's experience of these kinds of dialogues is presented by Tom Cosgrove, a progressive who put together a PBS documentary called, "Divided We

Fall: Unity without Tragedy," which features a diverse cross-section of Americans coming together to engage in civil discourse. The documentary spotlights GenXers and millennials on the left and right working, to see each other's perspectives and coming to a common understanding. The film pushes back on what Arthur C. Brooks has called our "culture of contempt," as the two groups came together, grappling with what it means to be an American, what divides us, and how to build bridges.[10]

Those are some optimistic antidotes to help combat cynicism. When we look for solutions to our vexing issues, we should look more toward the next generation than the next election cycle. Elected officials too often choose short-term stopgap answers to challenging social issues to appease their base rather than consider longer-range solutions.

Additional positive signs come from groups like the Problem Solvers Caucus, a group of Republican and Democratic congressional members who are seeking bipartisan solutions to break the current stubborn partisanship gridlock in our nation's capital. Another sign of forward-thinking can be found in political campaigns that focus on "solutions voters." The solutions voter is an optimistic person who believes that practical solutions can solve our problems. This engaged and informed constituency values practicality over dogma and compromise over confrontation. Solutions-oriented voters are willing to cross conservative and liberal lines on various positions. They act as a moderating force between dyed-in-the-wool liberals and staunch conservatives on many issues, ranging from immigration to criminal justice reform.

Solutions voters skew female, college-educated, Democratic, and under fifty years of age. These voters are more likely to choose solutions over ideology. Their voting choices are motivated by a candidate's position on a specific issue rather than their party affiliation or ideology. Another encouraging sign: polls show us that about one-third of Republicans are solutions-oriented.

In both parties, solution-oriented voters are more optimistic than ideology-driven voters, believing that contentious issues, such as affordable health care, are solvable. Unbound by ideology, they can move freely between conservative and liberal positions and are more open to ideas from anywhere along the political spectrum. When leaders offer solutions they can believe in, they will cross party lines—overcoming cynicism and restoring trust. Trust is essential for respect, and respect is the foundation we need. It must be. Before we can achieve those critical and worthy objectives, we need to delve even more deeply into the weeds. Let's look at the incentives presently keeping us so severely divided.

Chapter 3

Polarization: A Deep Dive into the Great Divide

K ristina Wilfore's story is an all-too-common example of what polarization looks like for many families today. As she related when we sat down to speak about these issues in the summer of 2021, "I was visiting my family for the first time since COVID-19 and was very excited—until the conversation turned extremely divisive and painful. I believe my dad is a radicalized type of person, and my sister and I have been at war with him since the election. Dad is an evangelical Christian and very conservative, so we are certainly on a different ideological path. Since my brother-in-law is Latino, my husband is Muslim, and my dad has four adopted grandchildren from China, our family dynamic should prioritize understanding in a man who is a proud, practicing Christian. Despite this, my father makes no connection to the disinformation against Muslims, Chinese people, and others."

"I always believed he is a good man, "Kristina said, "But now, he is a man I *used* to respect. The tension my sister and I had with my father came to a climax after the election, when we had to say, 'Enough is enough.' We tolerated his belief system for years, even though it hurt us. There were times we told him how it hurts us. Now, his refusal to accept the results of the election crossed an unacceptable line."

Kristina, one of Celinda's closest friends and colleagues, is an international political consultant who helps increase participation in parties and politics. She works with political leaders and NGOs throughout the United States, Europe, Africa, and the Middle East. She was the first executive director of the Ballot Initiative Strategy Center, awarded "The Most Valuable Think Tank" by *The Nation* magazine in 2009. She is currently working on a large-scale effort in the United States to respond to disinformation and understand its impact on the 2020 election. She has worked against the kind of authoritarian leaders in foreign countries that can emerge where division, distrust, inaction, and cynicism converge.

In this revealing conversation, Kristina sighed, took a deep breath, and continued to express her deep feelings on the issue at hand. "The whole question of polarization is so interesting to me," she said. "I would defer to you, Celinda, and to Ed to report on what your public opinion polls tell us. But I reject the notion some have that we are too divided to come together. Since the beginning of society, there has been polarization because differences of opinion are based on experience and vantage points. How the world looks to you shouldn't be a barrier to reconciling differences. There should be a way to have differences without everything being extreme and without a high stakes level of violence—for which there is zero gain. That is partly where we are because of disinformation and technology-driven information systems that are guiding much of the dialogue."

Kristina is correct that polarization is not new. Primary divisiveness about the role of government has echoed down the ages. Our brilliant Founding Fathers agreed to set up the Federal Republic based on a constitution. Their one stark difference of opinion centered on how powerful that Federal government should be.

Ideally, with determination, the gaps between these two opposing philosophies can continue to be bridged. A well-functioning Republic would feature open discussions and debates where people can understand one another and reach workable compromises. However, the current political environment is far from ideal, and what passes for compromise is the stubborn insistence on "doing it my way!"

Toxic polarization is causing havoc in politics and our lives. Many Americans view differences of opinion in politics as an assault on their way of life. Unwilling to compromise, they vilify the other side as a grave threat to their personal beliefs, their groups, and how they picture "their" United States. Party affiliation has become a significant part of many Americans' identities. Polite, respectful discourse, in which we listen and learn from each other, has fallen by the wayside.

Incivility, disrespect, and mistrust have trickled down from our public debates into our private conversations. As we saw in Kristina's situation, today's politics has taken on an almost religious fervor for some. For them, the morality of one's position leaves no room for the opposition to be anything but immoral. This attitude leads to contempt, fear, and the demonization of one's adversaries. In some ways, this current polarization is reminiscent of the great divide brewing before the Civil War, as it continues to test friendships and tear families apart.

Elected representatives often reflect this divide among their constituents. Many of them no longer look across the aisle to build bridges and reach common ground. Often, this leads to a standstill, where little gets done to move us forward in those critically essential core issues we discussed in the previous chapters.

Beneath it all, most Americans want the same basic bread and butter things: a good school for their children, the ability to buy a home, a decent salary, and the opportunity to enjoy their lives with their loved ones safely and peacefully. Interestingly, the percentage of American voters who define themselves as "politically moderate" has remained steadfast for decades. As have the "centrists," who say they are conservative or liberal but are not part of the far left or far-right ideologues who define themselves as "very" conservative or "very" liberal and are much louder in their public voice. Can this largely silent center be mobilized to break the gridlock in Washington? If we elect or select the kinds of leaders willing to respect differing views and look at changes that benefit everyone, we think so. To look at ways to help solve these challenges, we first need to look at *how* and *why* American politics and, as a result, the American public-at-large, ended up in this dire predicament. Jenny Eck, the progressive minority leader in the Montana State Legislature, always says, "Finding compromise does not mean being compromised." She put that to work in gaining bipartisan consensus on sexual harassment legislation.

How Did We Get Here?

Thomas Carothers and Andrew O'Donohue, Carnegie Endowment for National Peace Fellows, believe America's current polarization results from three major identity divisions: ethnic, religious, and ideological. They distinguish that in countries like Kenya and Rwanda, polarization comes from intense competition between ethnic groups and in India and Sri Lanka, the fractures are along religious lines. But here in the United States, they contend, all *three* of these divisions are involved. Thus, they say, our unique contentiousness in the areas of religion, race, and ideology makes our polarization virulent.

Another way to look at our polarization comes from retired college professor Robert Cushing and journalist Bill Bishop. In 2008, they coined the term "The Big Sort." Their book of the same name expresses their belief that we Americans are deliberately "sorting" ourselves into homogenous groups by moving into neighborhoods where we are surrounded by people who look, think, and sound like we do. This clustering together, they say, makes people who already hold similar views even *more* like-minded.

How "The Big Sort" continues to play out since 2008 is explored in a study published in 2016 in *Annals of American Association of Geographers* by co-authors Ron Johnston, David Manley, and Kelvyn Jones. As these authors noted, "There is clear evidence of significant spatial polarization of support for the country's two main political parties across recent presidential elections. Many people tend to vote the same way and tend to cluster together. Thus, such clustering increases, and the consequence is greater polarization in voting patterns."[11]

Americans *are* "sorting" ourselves in ways that go far beyond where we choose to live. We silo ourselves online and through the media that we consume. Facebook and Twitter show us that people prefer those with similar views *and* no longer want to influence other perspectives. It's a fact that most of us now get our news from sources that are skewed to further our existing worldviews.

This "sorting" also leads to uniformity on issues. For instance, few voters are likely to be both pro-life *and* pro-immigration. When voters sort themselves into ideological camps, they are less tolerant of divergent or competing groups. This ratchets up social tension, creating an "us versus them" mindset that moves us further from the fundamental economic, educational, and family-centric issues that need attention. It should be one of the most immediate concerns for Americans.

Where You Are in 'The Line'

As we said earlier, the burning question in American politics through the decades has been the same that once faced the Founding Fathers: What should the role of government be? Should the government play a limited role in our lives or a more expansive role in counterbalancing special interests and protect the rights of all individuals? Interestingly, our colleague, Mo Elleithee, looks at our division somewhat differently. He often publicly discusses his belief, with which we heartedly agree, that the paradigm has shifted from "Are you on the Left or the Right?"—or even "Are you liberal or conservative," to the metaphor of a hypothetical line. To him, the real question people are asking *themselves* today is, "Am I in the front or the back of that line?" For Mo, the line reflects that too many people feel the playing field is not level and that no matter how hard they work, they are constantly facing economic and social obstacles that hold them back. It shows that only when people feel they are being treated fairly and justly can there be widespread trust in our institutions and each other. What is fascinating about the front- or back-of-the-line way of describing a person's or group's ability to be seen and heard is that *everyone* feels, in some way, that they, or their community, are the ones stuck at the back, and that those at the front and their leaders are helping everyone else but them. Rural supporters tell us they feel left out in the cold by East Coast liberal elites who "clearly don't care about us." College-educated big-city liberals tell us that corporate greed and student loan debt, among other factors, make it impossible for them to live their American Dream. If, in truth, *everyone* feels like they are way in the back and there is no "justice" for them, it's not surprising that so many people have little interest in finding common ground.

As Mo reported in his Foreword, and as we continue to emphasize with specific details from recent history, the lack of trust in our institutions is largely responsible for the current polarization.

He points out that Obama's theme in 2008 of "hope and change" was aimed at the damage done to average Americans by special interests. A year later, in 2009, the Tea Party and the Occupy Movement arose, with the Tea Party going after Washington and the Occupy Movement going after Wall Street.

What Our Polls Tell Us

Data from one of our 2021 Battleground Polls highlights just how very polarized we have become. Undertaken in the early days of the Biden administration, it shows that, at that moment in time, a majority (56 percent) of voters thought the country was on the wrong track, including nine in ten Republicans (90 percent). And, in contrast, 73 percent of Democrats saw the country as headed in the *right* direction. As of June 2021, President Biden enjoyed almost universal *approval* among Democrats (96 percent). While 90 percent of Republicans disapproved of his job performance. Additionally, 85 percent of Democratic voters we polled approved of their Democratic congressional member, and a somewhat lower majority (55 percent) of Republicans supported their Republicans in Congress.[12]

One of the choices we have given subjects in our polls to grade overall performance was to rate leadership from the lowest level of "excellent," or 1 percent to the highest, 100 percent. Among Republicans, President Biden had a meager "excellent" score of 2 percent, while former President Trump had an "excellent" score of 37 percent. It's no surprise that the almost exact inverse was seen among Democrats, with President Biden's "excellent" score at 47 percent, while President Trump was given a mere "excellent" score of 2 percent.

In another joint Battleground poll we conducted, we gave voters nine key issues that span the policy spectrum. These included taxes, health care, immigration, race relations, and others. Asked if they thought the Democrats in Congress or the Republicans in Congress would better handle each of these issues, the striking finding was that 41 percent of the electorate, including 78 percent of Democrats, thought the GOP in Congress would not be able to do a better job on *any* of the issues. On the other side of the political aisle, 35 percent of the electorate, including 70 percent of Republicans, said the Democrats in Congress were no better at solving any issues. In other words, large majorities of voters in both the Democratic and Republican Parties believe the opposition party can no better handle even *one* of these nine key issues. This data dramatically shows that we are at odds with virtually *every* critical issue in this country.

Focus Groups Provide Insight

In May 2021, we conducted two Zoom focus groups of independent voters across fourteen "battleground" states—those states where the election could go either way and favor either a Democratic or Republican candidate. One focus group was composed of independent women who voted for Biden *but* voted for Trump in 2016 or whose partners voted for Trump in 2020. The other group consisted of independent senior male and female voters who voted for Trump in 2020 but felt (to varying degrees) somewhat conflicted about their vote. Interestingly, the group of women immediately took the conversation to COVID-19 before it went to politics—like the woman who felt shamed for wearing a mask in a grocery store. COVID-19 has only deepened and furthered polarization, a topic we deal with in detail in a later chapter.

These voters saw the Republican Party as in turmoil and more divided than the Democratic Party. At the same time, they saw *both* parties as divisive and mainly interested in power. They decried the lack of progress in Washington, DC, which they attributed in large part to an increasingly coarse and disrespectful political demeanor and dialogue between political leaders.

Several independent voters we polled suggested that Biden might be part of the solution to some of the divisions they saw in the government and the country, while others disagreed. Some voters saw the division in the government reflected in similar divisions in their own homes and workplaces—like Kristina Wilfore's experience with her father—and admitted to having had to put "no political discussions" rules in place with their families to avoid conflict.

When voters were asked whether they would prefer to have leaders who try to compromise, as opposed to those who stand firm on their values, our respondents struggled to answer the question. Many settled on saying they looked for leaders who knew when to compromise *and* still stand up for their beliefs. Issues seen as "compromise issues" included spending on infrastructure, while "standing your ground" topics included abortion and health care. Half of the independent voters who voted for Biden were divided about which party was more civil than the other but overall believed divisiveness came from both sides of the aisle. Here's what some of those independent voters had to say:

> *The Republicans just automatically naysay anything that the Democrats want. And I do feel that the Democrats are more open to listening, more open to talking about things.* (Independent Woman)

> *While it may be primarily on one side . . .*
> *It takes two to tango; it does.* (Independent Senior)

These independent voters blamed leaders across the political spectrum for the lack of civility in the government and the country. Voters tended to blame their candidate's opposing party for the rise in incivility.

Take this, for example:

> *Yeah [the liberals are contributing to lack of civility].*
> *The reason, yes, because of all these actions, it's not just one. All these actions that they're doing are contributing to the chaos.* (Independent Senior)

Unprompted, this group introduced into the discussion both "cancel culture" and ambivalence about what constitutes political correctness. These voters, especially Trump supporters and older voters, had significant concerns about how "cancel culture" contributes to division. There was a consensus among Trump voters that the return to civil conversations was essential for discussing their perspectives and beliefs without fear of being shamed. But these voters still felt that cancel culture was a key factor preventing these open conversations from happening. They saw this as making the path back to unity and mutual respect more difficult.

Below are some of their thoughts:

> *It's funny because you can't say anything. It's almost like you must have the same voice as maybe the Left. You have to have the same voice or else you [are] wrong.* (Independent Senior)

> *I'm sometimes feeling like my rights are kind of being taken away, and somebody else has control of our rights.* (Independent Senior)

> *It makes it almost impossible for you to be able to have a conversation with someone because they immediately think, well you're against me or you are racist.* (Independent Senior)

> *I think it's a whole culture. I think every topic that comes up always drives that line every time. You have to find, are you pro or against? Are you this, or are you that? And it's an extreme.* (Independent Woman)

When the topic of violence came up in these focus groups, they exhibited mixed feelings on their level of concern and what direction the violence was coming from. Trump voters were apprehensive about violence from liberals. They felt that while the actions of some groups (e.g., rioters from January 6) suffered legal consequences, others who had, to them, also committed acts of violence (e.g., Black Lives Matter protesters) were "getting away with it" by being seen as "peaceful protestors." Their thoughts below show their deep divisions:

> *The liberals come in and say, that's not a riot. That was just peaceful protesting, but they're in there stealing. There are pictures of it. . . .* (Independent Senior)

> *I think, being in Minneapolis, it's a perfect example of all the stuff going on. I mean, Minneapolis will never be the same as it was before.* (Independent Senior)

In this focus group, independents who voted for Biden showed more consensus that the violence was coming from conservatives or that both sides were guilty. These voters referenced the violence in Minneapolis (where one of the participants lived) but were far more worried about the January 6 insurrection. Voters in this group also felt violence was not anything new but that more attention was being paid to recent violence because of technological advancements in social media.

Their responses are illuminating:

> *I don't think that's a party thing. I think that's a people thing. I think there's going to be a violent group. I think that group changes depending on the atmosphere. But I think there's always a risk for violence.*
> (Independent Woman)

> *Think about the Civil Rights in the sixties—how much violence there was then. I mean, there's been violence all along with a lot of different things.* (Independent Woman)

*We had crazies bringing in scaffolding
to hang Mike Pence.* (Independent Woman)

Among all voters, there was *some* concern about a potential civil war. While voters did not feel a civil war was imminent, they did not rule it out as impossible. Biden voters referenced the insurrection as an example of why they felt a civil war was a distinct possibility. However, they did not reference the insurrection when addressing a possible civil war in the Trump group.

*I think people can only take so much. I mean, during it,
you're being told what to say or what you can say, that
sort of thing. I just don't think that people are going to
put up with it for an extended period.* (Independent Senior)

*I think it can get to that point. It might not be today,
tomorrow, or maybe not even our lifetimes. But it could
get to that point. I mean, we did in America before.*
(Independent Woman)

*I would hope not, but there is a chance of it. After the
insurrection.* (Independent Woman)

This group expressed frustration, believing that the government would tolerate violence if liberal causes perpetrated it.

*It seems like certain people in the government are
condoning violence and claiming it's peaceful. That's
really . . . All the riots in Portland, Seattle, Minneapolis
. . . The liberals come in and say, that's not a riot. . . . I*

mean, it's obvious they're condoning it to get their way.
(Independent Senior)

You know, it's funny because even in Columbus, the things that have happened in Columbus, and we're not that big of a city, and we're known to be very diverse. It's kind of a nice little melting pot, but at the same time, we've had riots downtown. They make you want to . . . we've got leaders, politicians that want to defund the police, and I don't even understand that. (Independent Senior)

Both groups agreed they wanted politicians to hold firm on some issues and compromise on other issues.

We need to compromise on the bills. There needs to be bipartisan working together to put the best budget, the best bills, the best everything together, that works for the most people . . . (Independent Senior)

Centrist Republicans and Democrats alike say they want to unite, but most voters on both sides, when asked directly, do not see it that way. Part of the problem, we believe, is that what people feel about their opponents is often an exaggerated version of reality; we tend to think the other side dislikes us and disagrees with us far more than they do.

Ways to Move Forward

Voters are showing signs they are tired of all the ugliness. They want to see more of what our leaders are for, not against. This optimistic attitude among voters should encourage politicians to embrace a new era of civility and respect. We urgently need a political strategy to provide voters with the two main things they want: unity and solutions. As our colleague, Mo Elleithee, says, "While congressional leaders in both parties debate bipartisanship and the importance of compromise, voters from both parties are pretty clear. They expect and demand results. In a contest between results and ideological purity, there is simply no contest."

So how *do* we get results? First, we need to acknowledge that essential connections and lines of communication between Democrats and Republicans have broken down. We need to agree that lawmakers must start talking to one another again instead of fighting back and forth on social media and in congressional chambers. These days, it is rare to see lawmakers socializing after work, or even eating together in the Capitol cafeteria, as they once did. Current misguided attempts at campaign finance reform have led to outlawing special interest groups from sponsoring getaways for elected officials and other leaders in a non-partisan environment. Equitable negotiations between people who have broken bread together have been replaced with stubbornness and finger-pointing. It is harder to vilify someone you had dinner with last night or someone with whom you've worked on an important social or political issue.

Democrats and Republicans have proven they *can* work together on shared interests. In one instance, both parties worked on legislation to improve the quality of foster care. The two co-sponsors of that legislation were Tom Delay, a conservative Texas Republican who has foster children, and Hillary Clinton when she was a Democratic senator. But a lot of water has gone under that bridge since that happened. Finding ways to interact together and look for common human interests will help decrease polarization.

Years ago, heavy schedules and long weeks in DC kept members of Congress in Washington much longer than they were at home. In many cases, they moved their families to Washington. When I was coaching basketball and baseball, I would get two or three of the politicians' kids on my teams. There would be a Democrat and a Republican, and they would go out together to root for their kids. That has completely changed. There is little to no family interaction these days.

When Newt Gingrich shortened the work week in Washington, members didn't have to come back in until Monday night and could leave Thursday night. The new schedule meant they had to squeeze all the DC fundraising into Tuesday, Wednesday, and Thursday nights. They would be working all day and fundraising all night, so having family sit and wait for them to come home late at night made no sense. That began the shift to their families not living in Washington, DC.

At the time, House Speaker Newt Gingrich explained he was trying to give politicians more time at home to campaign, fundraise, and, most importantly, be more connected with their constituents. Keeping their families at home in the congressional district made more sense. The strategy backfired, however, in the loss of healthy bipartisan togetherness. Another rift occurred when legislation banned conferences where Congress's Democrats and Republicans would spend a weekend together. The intention was to help keep elected officials from being influenced by special interest groups. However, this had the same unintended effect of preventing people with differing viewpoints from getting to know each other more respectfully.

The ability to discuss and debate differing opinions promotes an understanding of competing ideas. For example, some elected officials are more interested in championing reform and are more open to change, while others are far more comfortable with stability and tradition. A robust and responsive democracy needs resilience to change and a high level of stability. Democracy thrives when people with divergent views come together, negotiate their differences, and find solutions that benefit everyone. As Kristina asserted, the problem arises when we believe we are too divided to come together.

As we said at the outset, historically, some polarization is a constant. Differences of opinion are rooted in our divergent experiences and vantage points. But how the world looks to you or us should not be a barrier to reconciliation. Finding common ground through shared values will remove all or at least most of the polarizing issues that now leave us prone to inaction. Even worse, the current standoff leaves us vulnerable to high-stakes violence, as we see, week after week and month after month, somewhere in our country.

There have been encouraging signs that we may not be as polarized on things that matter as it appears on the surface. One such encouraging sign showed up in a July 2014 meta-study by the University of Maryland's Center on Policy Attitudes. That study compared responses to 388 polling questions from various polls asked of voters in both red and blue states. In two-thirds of the answers, the study found no statistical differences in positions between Democrats and Republicans. Topics with no significant polarization ranged from affordable housing to raising taxes and social security. The American public has many shared interests not based on ideology but common sense. Still, in recent years, those common interests seem increasingly lost in Washington, DC's highly charged partisan political environment.

The Polarizing Filibuster

The 60 Vote Rule in the Senate is also known as "the filibuster." Before a bill can pass, a total of sixty of the one hundred Democratic and Republican senators must agree. Requiring such a large number makes it almost impossible to obtain a majority vote and usually blocks *any* legislation. The filibuster thus effectively suppresses dialogue and compromise.

The filibuster gets its name from Senate Rule XXII, allowing a senator to speak as long as they want until sixty of one hundred senators vote to close the debate. In support of the filibuster, the minority party can force the majority party—the one in power— to negotiate with them. Even if all fifty senators from the majority party vote in unison, in most sessions of Congress, *some* opposition party votes would still be needed to reach sixty and pass any legislation. In recent years, the lock-step style of partisanship has moved both parties away from the give-and-take compromise, which is supported by a full 70 percent of the electorate. This is where legislators could garner some opposite party votes and get things done. Without this willingness to compromise, important legislation languishes in gridlock. George Washington's comment was about the Senate as a legislative body designed to let the "tea cool." Today, the Senate is where legislation not just cools off but gets ice cold.

We both want reforms in this area that would make action possible. For Celinda, the answer is to reduce the necessary votes to fifty, thereby ending the filibuster. While Ed agrees that reforming the filibuster is urgent, he sees no need to change the number of votes needed from sixty to fifty. Instead, he proposes requiring each senator from each party to answer their question with a simple yes or no to this question: "Do you want to take up legislation to address this issue or concern?"

Let's say the bill was on infrastructure. If more than sixty of the one hundred senators say, "Yes, I do want this issue to be addressed by the Senate in this legislative session." Then the "super majority's" vote would assign the issue to the appropriate committee(s) to begin the process of writing the legislation. The devil will always be in the details, but at least they start the process with agreement on the common ground that makes any reasonable changes possible. It takes away the traditional attack by Democrats on Republicans when dealing with legislation where they question the "intention" of Republicans rather than the bill's merits. The question might be how much funding to allocate to repair our crumbling roads, bridges, eroding shorefronts, and other failing parts of our infrastructure. For Ed, both parties agreeing that this challenge *should* be addressed would eliminate the need for a filibuster on the final passage.

One beautiful example of a respectful exchange between two people with different political views is a conversation the then sixteen-year-old Mo Elleithee had when he met John McCain. Mo kept this exchange private until August 24, 2018—the day before Senator McCain died. Knowing the end was near, Mo decided to tweet his conversation with McCain, a remarkable war hero and public servant whom he deeply respected despite their widely differing views on many issues.

At sixteen, I got to meet Sen. John McCain for the first time.

Me: "I'm honored to meet you even though I disagree with you."

McCain responded: "Well, I'm honored to represent you even though you disagree with me."

Mo found the comments (tweets) made under his post heartening. One user said it was a good day to put differences aside in the name of peace. Another Twitter account holder said the exchange brought him to tears while he was at lunch, admitting that even though he didn't vote for Senator McCain, he always respected him.

These exchanges, among many similar tweets, give us hope. It shows that people *are* hungry for respect to reappear in politics and life. They are eager for us to put our petty differences aside in favor of the common good. Hope springs eternal, but we genuinely believe there *is* hope for finding a way to work together. We Americans have many shared values that can be put into play to unite us. As Americans, we should be tired of the political divisions threatening our democracy.

In our many years as pollsters, we've discovered there are large numbers of more moderate, *centrist* voters, and they do not act as a block. But many voters are flexible in their views and will willingly cross party lines. They are likely to hold what some may see as contradictory opinions across the political spectrum. For instance, unlike many on the far right and far left, they *can* be pro-life and pro-immigration or pro-abortion and pro-gun. Those in the center often go unheard because they are not as active or well-funded as the extremists on the far right and far left and thus less attractive to media outlets—an issue of incentives we will discuss in a later chapter.

Since members of this group of centrist voters do not share their party's line on every issue, they are the most open to compromise. Voters in this category respect the core values that are the foundation of our nation's belief systems. They think we should listen to the other side and compromise instead of stubbornly sticking to our often-inherited beliefs and fighting each other. They look for a path forward that builds upon our democratic heritage of faith, trust, and cooperation.

We each hold strong opinions and see nothing wrong with feeling strongly about one's party on a given issue or cause. Quite the contrary; throughout history, those with passion and purpose are often those very dedicated visionaries and activists that have created positive change.

But with urgent challenges facing us, there is no time to lose. Right now, we must strive to make the world a better place for us, our children, and their children, all of whom will inherit what we leave them. We both confess to being optimists. Hopefully, as you delve more deeply into this book, you, too, will see why we believe in the essential goodness of people and share our confidence that working together, we can usher in a new era of civility built on a foundation of trust and respect.

Chapter 4

Toxic Incentives: Bad Behavior Richly Rewarded

The principle that Americans reward virtuous behavior is a foundational tenet of our nation. We all believe—or claim to—that good deeds, honesty, hard work, and respect are to be championed and accompanied by success. Our laws, social norms, and moral codes are also supposed to hold bad actors accountable. Sadly, that is often not the case today. Polarizing, divisive language and behavior from institutions and influential individuals are often met with monetary and political gain. America is increasingly trapped in a broken incentive structure.

The Current Incentive Structure

Think of this current "structure" as the very opposite of the values taught in our schools, places of worship, and households. This structure rewards polarization. Some politicians turn finding common ground into a negative and use vicious attacks to motivate voters. Online, shoddily reported stories still attract thousands or even tens of thousands of clicks. On cable news, false "hot takes" by vitriolic pundits are watched by millions every evening. This avalanche of viewers and clicks brings in ad revenue and followers and the motivation to continue the cycle.

This cycle of polarizing rhetoric is driven forward, in large part, by the media, by cynical politicians, and by tech giants motivated by attracting dollars rather than by producing respectful dialogues. These institutions and individuals perpetuate this incentive structure in two main ways:

1. They surrender to it. Some political leaders throw up their hands and say, "I can't overcome this, so I'm going to go along for the ride." They sell what people buy, even if the product sows discord amongst their electorate.

2. They stoke the flames of polarization. They exacerbate divides because there is both a political and a financial benefit. They worsen problems for their gain. Rather than addressing the issue, some institutions fuel it because of the economic and political incentives.

Large tech companies engage in this practice, mainly on their social media sites. We will comprehensively address social media's threat in *Chapter 6, Not So Social Media: Repairing a Once Promising Connectivity.* It bears mentioning here that many social networking sites are also market-driven and reactive. Instead of upholding principles, they feed base instincts. A September 2021 study from NYU's Center for Business and Human Rights, titled "Fueling the Fire: How Social Media Intensifies U.S. Political Polarization—And What Can Be Done About It," concluded that "social media platforms are not the main cause of rising partisan hatred, but the use of these platforms intensifies divisiveness and thus contributes to its corrosive effects."[13]

Social media companies are tight-lipped about how their algorithms can rank, recommend, and remove content. Such transparency would open them to criticism about how hate speech and extreme political infighting contribute to their advertising revenue. Those earnings are *massive* and only growing. In the first quarter of 2021, Facebook's net income rose 94 percent to $9.5 billion, up from $4.9 billion in the first quarter of 2020. Facebook reported revenue of $26.17 billion, up 48 percent compared with the prior year.

Elected officials throw kindling on an already burning fire by profiting from racist, anti-Semitic, Islamophobic, or sexist rhetoric. In March 2021, social media posts written by Republican Georgia Representative Marjorie Taylor Greene claimed, among other things, that a Jewish space laser started the 2018 California wildfires. The story immediately went viral. Greene has also expressed views that leading Democratic officials should be executed, that Muslims don't belong in government, and that Zionist supremacists are masterminding Muslim immigration to Europe.

Why should any *one* of these views be publicly aired? Each one should have disqualified a representative from being trusted with public service. Greene used the controversy she created to her advantage by doubling down, motivating her supporters to come to her aid. On April 7, 2021, *Forbes* reported that just a month after her comments surfaced, Greene had "raised $3.2 million in the first quarter of 2021."[14] That's a staggering sum, especially for a freshman member of Congress, and one that suggests her marginalization in Congress has not "dented her brand." As far as money is concerned, her "brand" is stronger than ever. As of September 2021, Greene is the top Republican fundraiser in the House of Representatives.

Paul Gosar is a congressman from Arizona, the same state where Congresswoman Gabrielle Giffords was shot in an act of senseless political violence. Gosar seemingly forgot that important history when in November 2021, he posted a digitally edited clip of an anime cartoon, in which his "character" slashes Representative Alexandria Ocasio-Cortez to pieces with swords. It also showed him lunging violently at President Biden. It was a bizarre action from a sitting congressman, but what occurred after was even more unsettling. Democrats were rightly outraged. California Representative Ted Lieu stated, "In any workplace in America, if a coworker made an anime video killing another coworker, that person would be fired."[15]

Lieu was right, and Twitter flagged the post as "hateful," but Gosar doubled down. "The depiction of Mr. Biden pertains to his administration's decision to leave the border open while illegal aliens invade from all points," Gosar retorted. He even called illegal immigration a "plague." This level of rhetoric, combined with violent imagery, reeks of extremism.[16]

The House of Representatives moved swiftly, passing legislation that censured Gosar and stripped him of his two committee assignments. It was the first time a sitting House member had been censured in more than ten years.

But Gosar wasn't finished. Precisely *one hour* after being censured, a time when a leader should have been looking inward and reassessing his behavior, Gosar retweeted the video. It was an extremely aggressive move, one that leapfrogged over a line of respectful discourse that had long been crossed.

The actions of one bad actor are understandable, but what troubles us most about this situation is that Gosar wouldn't have acted in this manner if he wasn't incentivized to do so. Gosar was applauded by many, and his Twitter followers increased. His base, many of whom support conspiracy theories like QAnon, were feeding off the chum he'd thrown in the water. He was referred to as a champion of free speech by some. Perhaps the address should be protected but praising him as some hero for posting the video is a far cry from asserting his right to post it. Our broken incentive structure, once again, worked against the benefit of all but the most extreme, violent voices.

These are two of the more egregious cases of politicians "fanning the flames." Still, they indicate broader problems that have been developing for some time on both ends of the political spectrum. One classic example is Congresswoman Maxine Waters, who, in her first term in Congress, called President George H. W. Bush a racist.[17] In 1994, she had to be formally reprimanded and was suspended from the House floor for repeatedly interrupting another member who was speaking. She accused the CIA of selling crack cocaine in her district. (The US Department of Justice and *The Los Angeles Times* found no evidence to support this claim.)[18]

Waters voted to object to the certification of the GOP presidential winner in 2000, 2004, and 2016. In 2018, she said, "If you see anybody from [Trump's] Cabinet in a restaurant, in a department store, at a gasoline station, you get out, and you create a crowd, and you push back on them, and you tell them they're not welcome anymore, anywhere."[19]

Speaking of pushing back, Alan Grayson, a Florida Democrat now running for the Senate, was proud to call himself a "potential brawler." Grayson dominated nightly talk shows with statements like, "Republicans want you to die quickly," and raised huge sums of money for his campaign from small donors. He established fundraising techniques that other prominent Democrats have used.[20]

On both sides of the aisle, polarizing and disrespectful behavior is incentivized and protected. People can make strong critiques of each other's ideology and actions. In many ways, the significant difference in the inflammatory rhetoric of politicians of the past and those of the current moment lies with our current incentive structure within social media and cable news networks.

Our current incentive structure is rooted in the polarization and the cynicism we examined in Chapters Two and Three. If these behaviors continue to intensify and be rewarded, they will only worsen our cynicism, polarization, and alienation from one another politically and socially over time. Unless we learn to incentivize *respect*, our national divide will continue to widen, harming everyone and weakening the foundation of our society in every arena.

In many ways, the significant difference in the inflammatory rhetoric of Congresswoman Maxine Waters over the last thirty years and Congresswoman Marjorie Taylor Greene over the previous thrity months on their unethical and uncivil behavior with our current incentive structure within social media and cable news networks are on steroids.

Why *do* Americans continue to participate, sometimes enthusiastically, in this broken system? Part of the problem is biological. In a 2019 article, University of California's Davis campus psychology professor Alison Ledgerwood, who studies framing effects—how people process information based on how it's presented to them—explained that our brains are hard-wired to seek out and remember negative information. "A negative frame is much more persistent, or 'stickier' than a positive one," she wrote.[21]

Let's take the example of negative campaign ads. Everyone says they don't like negative ads, yet they are often very effective. "That fact isn't lost on politicians and political parties," Ledgerwood wrote. "Once a negative idea has been planted, it's tough to shake. If you come at an issue negatively but are later reminded of the policy's positive aspects, you will still think it's a bust."

Rewarding negativity erodes our private lives as well as our public discourse. In our Battleground Poll, we consistently see data that shows this problem causes many Americans to feel helpless and unhappy. The Founding Fathers foresaw this long ago. "The diminution of public Virtue is usually attended with that of public Happiness," wrote Samuel Adams in a letter dated April 30, 1776.[22]

Our joint focus groups also show that people are increasingly frustrated with incentivizing poor practices. Many people we interviewed had no solutions to offer, particularly women's group voters we talked to.

These voters felt strongly that division in the country was a big problem but were unsure what—if anything—could remedy the situation. They saw this polarization as a significant impediment to progress in Washington and believed the problem was getting worse. Many of the participants who said they were independents saw former President Donald Trump as a significant player exacerbating this dynamic. Still, he was far from the only guilty party in these voters' eyes; likewise, they took issue with the media, including social media, and with individual politicians.

The Public's Responsibility

Mo Elleithee feels that part of the problem lies with the public's reactions. He frequently poses the question: "How do our political institutions try to move forward when they are often penalized by voters for demonstrating respect?" We agree. Much of the country *says* we should be less polarized and treat each other with dignity, understanding, and open minds. Yet, a large portion of the public still incentivizes terrible behavior. They still watch the border-line demagoguery of political pundits each night on their favorite channels and shows. They still vote for candidates who continue to appeal to our worst instincts, candidates who seldom work to motivate respect and instead incentivize political institutions from moving us toward a better place.

We feel that while institutions and public figures shoulder much of the blame since they often choose to surrender to it or actively fuel the flames, the public certainly has a moral and civic duty not to incentivize bad behavior.

People can choose to circumvent this toxic incentive structure individually and in their groups. Our society can respond to integrity and goodness from our leaders. We've seen it countless times throughout American history. Earlier in the chapter, we talked about how negative campaign ads stick in people's minds. But some candidates have found a way around that obstacle simply by being original and honest. John Hickenlooper, United States senator from Colorado, has *never* run negative ads in his entire career, making many campaign managers roll their eyes. During his 2010 bid for governor of the state, he managed to break through to the public with an ad still being discussed in political circles today, even if it's with a chuckle.[23]

Hickenlooper climbs into the shower in a hit TV spot—fully clothed in a business suit. As the water rains down on him, he looks up at the camera and says, "I'm John Hickenlooper. And I guess I'm not a very good politician because I can't stand negative ads. Every time I see one, I feel like I need to take a shower, and you see *a lot* of them. With all the challenges we face, Colorado needs a governor who brings people together, creates jobs and government spending. That's why I won't run negative ads. Pitting one group against another or one part of Colorado against another doesn't help anyone. And besides, we need the water." Then the shower sprays him directly in the face. This ad was enormously popular, and Hickenlooper won the election. Hickenlooper didn't give in to negativity, and the public took notice.

Below, Ed gives his thoughts on the times, throughout his long career, that he's seen the circumvention of toxic incentive structures make a real difference.

Positive and the Art of Political Jiu-Jitsu

It bothers me when people say, "I don't like negative campaigns, but they work." Although the statement is true, it doesn't *have* to work. People do not inherently gravitate toward the negative. And you can win if you can find a way *around* it.

I've worked as a pollster and strategist on many tightly contested races. In recent years, the first thing the campaign does is an opposition research project on the opponent—the ultimate search for the wedge that can be driven between the opponent and the voters. I prefer to spend the early part of the campaign looking for the magnet to attract and pull voters to my candidate. To the extent possible, I like to have the candidate spend several months driving around the district and taking notes about their observations of the people. Observe the kinds of houses and neighborhoods people live in and even take a ride down their Main Street. Have a meal in a local diner and listen to the conversations and debates over pancakes and eggs. The purpose was to start the campaign by connecting the dots between my candidate and voters and what they had to offer voters to meet their needs.

Even when my candidate is attacked in speeches, sound bites, and ads, my first response is not to up the ante and retaliate in kind. I think of my strategy as a game of political jiu-jitsu. Jiu-jitsu revolves around the concept that a smaller, weaker person can successfully defend themselves against a bigger, stronger, heavier opponent by using leverage. Sometimes, the best response is to turn their negativity against them. I remember employing this strategy when I served as pollster and strategist in Haley Barbour's 2003 gubernatorial campaign in Mississippi. He was running both for the first time and against the incumbent governor. Our focus groups found that the current governor was often seen as overstating his accomplishments and understating his inadequacies. We felt they would go after Haley Barbour in the media, saying Haley was head of Washington's number one lobbying group.

Our focus groups convinced Haley Barbour to let his opponent run his mouth. What we needed was patience. Patience to give them enough rope to where they crossed the line. Barbour had the guts, and he drove the timing of the plan. We didn't respond when they ran the first of their negative campaign ads. Sure enough, after four days, they pulled that spot and took it up a notch! They went from Haley having hurt everyone from seniors to children to workers in the first ad to a follow-up ad that positioned Haley as sending jobs from Mississippi to Mexico, letting children go hungry, and killing Mississippi seniors from neglect. That's when Barbour said: "Okay, now's our time."

The morning after this new ad ran, we held a press conference. Barbour walked to the podium and declared, "You know, they're right. I have the number one lobbying firm in Washington, and if you hire me to be your governor, I will put *you* number one also." As a result, we went from five points down to five points ahead in a matter of days and held the lead for the rest of the campaign. Then we won. We had used the negativity and overreach in their ads and turned them into a positive. The electorate rewarded us for that. Today, it worries me deeply that such a wide swath of the American public responds so enthusiastically to divisive rhetoric. I'm disappointed in the institutions that perpetuate this cycle. Yet, just like my father, I remain an eternal optimist. By appealing to the better angels of our nature, I believe we can reverse this tide.

Current United States Secretary of Transportation and Mayor Pete Buttigieg did just that during his 2020 presidential run. Back then, Buttigieg was the mayor of a small city called South Bend, Indiana. Few people had heard of Buttigieg or South Bend. Then he did something that made me, and many other Americans, take notice. In the early days of his campaign, Buttigieg personally drafted his "Rules of The Road."[24] They were a set of principles that would guide his campaign staffers and volunteers through what promised to be one of the most ruthless Democratic primaries in recent memory. Buttigieg's rules were: *Boldness, Belonging, Teamwork, Discipline, Excellence, Substance, Respect, Responsibility, Truth,* and *Joy.* He had each of his staffers sign the document as a pledge to uphold these values and had copies distributed to be read by all of his volunteers.

The document moved me, and the man gained my respect. While other candidates were on the campaign trail slinging mud, Buttigieg was appealing to Americans' better angels. His text is too long to repeat here in total, but I'll share three of my favorite Rules of the Road.

RESPECT: *In our thoughts, words, and actions, we cultivate a sense of respect. We respect one another on this team; we respect the office of the Presidency, and we respect every individual we encounter on the campaign trail, including our competitors. The* *better we hold up this value among ourselves, the better it will reflect outside. It will represent a quiet antidote to the idea that this project is too audacious to be taken seriously.*

TRUTH: *Honesty is in our nature. It is one of our most important means of restoring faith in our democracy among everyday Americans and building a national movement rooted in trust and faith in our country and beliefs. Internally and externally, our effort will be characterized by fidelity to the truth.*

RESPONSIBILITY: *The conduct of a campaign can be as influential as its outcome. Everyone on this team has a responsibility to live up to our values, and every participant, from a first-time volunteer to the candidate and top staff, must model this. When there is a mistake, we take ownership, learn, adjust, and move on. Missteps are inevitable, but they should never be repeated. We own our choices and our work.*

Impressed, I called Buttigieg's Iowa State director a month before the election. She answered the phone at 10 p.m. and talked with me for an hour and a half. She was proud of what they'd put together and was excited that a Republican pollster would call her to speak openly. It was a moment of connection across the aisle, spurred on by positivity.

As you know, Buttigieg did not become the president of the United States—but his steadfast commitment to values has made him a national figure with a massive following of young voters. A large part of the electorate valued his philosophy. It's an example of the right kind of incentive structure that I, an eternal optimist, believe *can* still exist in America.

A Final Case Study on Valuing Virtue

One final case study from many in our country's history shows how virtue won over division. It was the cold winter of 1968, and as the Vietnam War raged on, Robert F. Kennedy visited the Appalachian region of eastern Kentucky. Appalachia, one of the nation's poorest areas, had been economically devastated for decades by a coal mining industry that exploited workers. According to journalist Peter Edelman, Appalachia was plagued by "a local power structure committed to perpetuating itself at all costs, and unwilling to countenance the slightest improvement in the lives of the excluded, for fear they would gain the confidence and the wherewithal to overturn the status quo at the ballot box."[25] Doesn't that sound distressingly similar to the problems our society faces today?

The official purpose of Kennedy's visit was to judge the impact of President Lyndon Johnson's "War on Poverty." Kennedy found that deep problems remained. However, he felt he wasn't there to stir political anger against a future opponent. He was there to listen to the people. He met with dozens of families throughout his trip, spoke to huge crowds, and answered questions, taking in their everyday concerns.

Even people with a deeply held distrust of politicians welcomed him with open arms. Author Matthew Algeo, in his book, *All This Marvelous Potential: Robert Kennedy's 1968 Tour of Appalachia,* writes, ". . . the people of the region remember RFK's as being the most meaningful, the most understanding, and the best listener. People often cite his large family, his warmth, and his genuine concern when they talk about his effect on them and speak of the way he brought hope."[26]

In our current era of seemingly insurmountable divides, we must look for hope anywhere we can find it. The two of us believe that mutual respect is an essential starting point. Robert Kennedy himself once said, "All of us might wish at times that we lived in a more tranquil world, but we don't. And if our times are difficult and perplexing, so are they challenging and filled with opportunity."[27]

We certainly do not live in a *tranquil* America. And we, your authors, certainly don't profess to have all the solutions to our nation's problems. We aren't naïve enough to think that a single book can turn around a toxic incentive structure that has been in place for decades. Here is our belief: restoring respect can—and will—move the needle further toward our shared values.

Part Two
Building Bridges

Chapter 5

Problem-Solving Strategies:
Workable Solutions for a New Era

I n the first half of this book, we made our case why Americans are polarized and cynical and why we seem to lack basic respect for one another. We've outlined our broken incentive structure and shown why many political solutions don't address foundational issues. Now that we've identified these issues and given some insight into how they function in American society, it's time to think about *fixing* them.

That is going to need a great deal of problem-solving. It's going to require drawing on the lessons of the past—while looking ahead for bold strategies that can define our new era. It's also going to necessitate an understanding of problem-solving: what works, why it works, and how it can be applied pragmatically to the significant challenges our nation is facing.

For sure, it's an uphill battle. We know America's issues can't be solved overnight. We certainly don't think that all of the answers can be found within the pages of this or any single book.

Despite our best intentions and desires, we can't make rural and urban Americans suddenly start liking each other. We can't pretend there aren't real divides in this country that may divide us for a long, long time.

We also know that the political class has a choice. They—and we—can capitulate to this grim state of affairs or try to figure out ways around it. This chapter offers strategies we've gleaned from our long careers in which we gathered and studied voter data and having both had a front-row vista on how Washington politics function. We've seen what works, and we've seen what doesn't. Hopefully, we can impart some of what we've learned along the way.

When trying to solve a complex problem, the name of the game is progress, not perfection. Effective strategies usually have one of three components.

1. They use discourse to get to the heart of an issue.
2. They are based on mutual respect, especially among unlikely allies.
3. They prioritize solutions over ideology.

Beyond Ideology

Let's examine that word *ideology*. Traditionally, it's defined as a firm set of political ideas that, with us Americans, usually fall into one of these two categories: liberal or conservative. Those are complex identities rooted in cultural allegiances, geographic locations, and familial histories. A cattle rancher from West Texas will likely identify as conservative, just as schoolteachers from Seattle will probably proudly proclaim that they are liberal.

Unfortunately, these ideological identities often prevent Americans from seeing the other side. They act as barriers to communication, which is the all-important first step toward solving a problem. If you think of someone's belief system as totally antithetical to your own, it's much more difficult to dialogue with them, even if that is not the truth of the matter. Suppose Americans perceive someone as a "socialist" or a "fascist," two words that get thrown around and misused far too often these days. In that case, urgently needed progress on real issues is hobbled by a depth of ideological distance caused by fear and resentment.

Interestingly, when pressed on what's important to them, most Americans are not ideologues. We see this again and again in our Battleground Polls. Americans may, for a variety of different reasons, *say*, "I'm conservative" or "I'm liberal," but that doesn't mean they're ideologically conservative or liberal. The chances are more likely that the cattle rancher from West Texas and the schoolteacher living in the Pacific Northwest want the same basic things for themselves and their families. Just as likely, they aren't too concerned about what political theory achieves that goal. The *goal,* the final result, is the crucial thing. Voters over the last decade believe that any three people in America can agree on more than the two parties in Congress do.

So what *are* Americans if not ideological? We are pragmatists. Yet, the way we discuss far too many problems is along ideological lines. We shouldn't. Most problems don't have anything to do with ideology, and we should stop thinking about them through those lenses. That *will* mean reaching into uncomfortable places and forming alliances that might at first feel strange. But if, as a result, problems get solved, we believe Americans will forgo their supposed ideologies for these desired results to our common fundamental issues.

"Problem Solvers" Attempt to Solve Root Problems

Among the many serious repercussions in the weeks and months after the January 6, 2021 insurrection, the dense clouds of mistrust got everyone questioning everyone else, including both inner and inter-party factions.

Even during the darkest days, one group of lawmakers quietly worked to get things done. While others attacked each other verbally, The Problem Solvers Caucus, a fifty-six-member bipartisan group in the House, drafted legislation designed to solve one major root problem: our nation's crumbling infrastructure. Throughout the spring, The Problem Solvers met with the White House and the Senate, focusing on productive results rather than on personalities or making political points.

Indeed, it would be remiss *not to* mention this caucus, and its history, in a chapter devoted to problem-solving. Although The Problem Solvers were officially formed in 2017, they started their work back in 2013 when a group of seventy congresspeople—roughly a fifty-fifty split between Democrats and Republicans—banded together to introduce nine bills designed to "make government more efficient, effective and less wasteful." They dubbed themselves "The Problem Solvers." As Rep. John Barrow (D-GA) said at the time, "In Washington, compromise has become a dirty word. Working together to get things done is a big breath of fresh air for the American people."[28]

Particularly in the last five years, The Problem Solvers have been a force for pragmatic bi-partisanship. In a co-headlined op-ed for *The New York Times* on August 4, 2017, co-leaders Josh Gottheimer (D-NJ) and Tom Reed (R-NY) wrote: "We have contrasting ideas—one of us is a Democrat, the other a Republican—about what ails the system and how to reshape it. But this is not the time for more partisan fighting. It's time to build a better system, even if incrementally because that's what the American people deserve."[29]

And, too rare on The Hill, The Problem Solvers have followed the principles they espouse in the press more often than not. They've crafted and helped pass solid bipartisan legislation on health care and COVID-19 relief and have reformed the rules of the House in an attempt to "break the Gridlock." You'll notice that all of these efforts seek to cure a root problem in our society. We find this time and time again in our Battleground Poll: Americans want these issues *resolved*. They don't particularly care about the ideology behind the solutions, so long as the outcome materially improves their lives.

It hasn't always been easy. Even the road to the 2021 infrastructure bill, called "The Infrastructure Investment and Jobs Act," was rife with dramatics. Both Democrats and Republicans from the far ends of the political spectrum threatened to tank it. But The Problem Solvers knew that America needed to build bridges and modernize airports. They also knew we needed to rebuild the electric grid and expand broadband internet access. Voting for the bill meant defying party leadership in favor of doing what they thought was suitable for the American public. That takes courage. That takes caring about your constituents more than your political career. That takes a desire to actually solve problems, not just pay lip service to your base. The infrastructure bill passed because it was something the majority of the American public wanted and every state urgently needed.

What's critical to us is that while The Problem Solvers don't agree on everything and may vote differently from time to time, they respect Americans enough to focus their efforts on root problems. The government will never be a perfect entity, but we believe that when our leaders act in good faith, the public will sense that, and trust will grow. Trust is the seed of healing we desperately need when our nation finds itself at a dangerous crossroads, and trust is built, first and foremost, on a willingness to respect our differences as well as those areas where we agree.

Ed Making "Unlikely Allies" Work

Whenever I think about problem-solving strategies, I return to the relationship I enjoy with Celinda. Some might consider us unlikely allies. We have very different ideas about the government's role in people's lives. That isn't the foundation of our professional partnership or our friendship. The key to our relationship is that, from the very beginning, we took away the need to show how we contrast each other or make apologies for our differences. Because we have mutual respect, we are free to say what we think, even when we disagree.

We have often challenged each other. We've even disagreed on how to write this book. Yet, this is a source of strength in our relationship. We respect each other enough to communicate with respect because we have a common goal: to help find workable solutions. That openness lets us see that our ultimate commitments are the same.

I'll give you an example of when Celinda and I faced a bump, solved the problem, and used it to strengthen our bond. The disagreement occurred in 2008, going into the first Obama campaign. The Democrats were very hot about messaging, accusing Republicans of trying to suppress votes. I felt Celinda was too vocal on this subject in a way that wasn't productive, especially since we were conducting a massive poll together. I raised the point to her that stating her judgments so firmly put me in a position to defend my party against the accusations.

Instead of letting this ideological rift come between us, we sat down and talked it out. I gave her my point of view, and she gave me hers. I asked her to soften her stance by not making a blanket statement that *all* Republicans intended to suppress voters. I explained how, from my side of the aisle, I saw Democrats engaging in some nefarious practices of their own, trying to steal or manufacture votes, but never in either a big way or driven by either the campaigns or the Democratic Party itself. At the same time, I took a hard look at what my side was doing. *Did* some types of voter suppression occur? In some isolated cases, the answer was yes. Not in a central, organized way, by either the Republican Party or the campaigns themselves, but there are always bad actors thinking they are helping their candidate win. In our conversations about this issue, I equated it to people who tore down the opponent's yard signs, thinking that would help win the election. My point was that these actions are not done universally on *either* side but rather are done by a few bad actors and that this has little to no impact on the actual result of the election.

To her great credit, Celinda was open to this dialogue. We achieved a respectful resolution because we wanted the same thing: free and fair elections. Celinda's analysis was tempered by these discussions in our Battleground Poll that fall. To be sure, she said her piece, but respectfully, making my voice heard. I did the same. Twelve years later, we are still working together, debating, and solving problems—unlikely allies, to be sure, but partners and supporters just the same.

Improbable partnerships can lead to unique solutions outside of the structural thinking we need right now. I'll give you an example of how this can occur nationally. You wouldn't necessarily expect Hillary Clinton to work hand-in-hand with former Republican Minority Whip Tom Delay of Texas and business leader Dave Thomas of Wendy's, a diehard conservative. Yet that's precisely what happened in 1997 when Clinton was First Lady. The three of them found they had a common goal: to solve the root problem of children living in unfit homes and dangerous foster care programs.

In 1997, this unlikely trio helped craft and passed the "Adoption and Safe Families Act of 1993," which provided support and services for adoptive families. By 2002, foster adoptions had increased by 64 percent. A January 1998 *Washington Post* piece called the law "the most significant change in federal child-protection policy in almost two decades."[30] The three didn't stop there, continuing to help push through the Foster Care Independence Act of 1999, which focused on children who "age out" of the foster care system when they turn eighteen. Both bills are widely viewed as successful bi-partisan efforts that have helped hundreds of thousands of children.

In another example of two unlikely allies coming together to solve a problem, there's the example of Senators Joni Ernst (R-Iowa) and Kirsten Gillibrand (D-NY). When Gillibrand was still in the presidential race, she endorsed Ernst's 2020 primary opponent. Ernst shrugged it off and did not let it stop her from supporting a bipartisan bill to help prevent sexual assault in the military that Gillibrand helped champion. The bill was passed earlier this year by the Senate Armed Services Committee. This bill, the "Military Justice Improvement and Increasing Prevention Act," is landmark legislation that has the support of over sixty-five senators, and Ernst and her colleagues are calling for a Senate floor vote on the full measure.

Celinda: Let's Look at Examples by Determined Women

Agreeing with everything Ed just said, I want to continue this line of thinking by examining practical problem-solving examples from those who, historically, have been shut out of the discussion or actively suppressed. As a woman in polling, a male-dominated profession, I believe diversity, including gender diversity, should always be part of how we can effectively navigate to reach a workable compromise. You can't weigh in if you don't have a seat at the table! But when that seat at the table is offered, or in most cases fought for, tremendous progress can occur.

In the late fall of 2013, the government found itself on the precipice of a prolonged shutdown. Talks had stalled on both sides of the aisle over the usual issue: the budget. Neither side seemed willing to bend as the American public grew increasingly frustrated, and rightly so. People want their tax dollars to go to programs and policies, not wasted by quibbling along party lines. After weeks of getting nowhere, a group of women in Congress decided to take action. Republican Senators Susan Collins of Maine, Lisa Murkowski of Alaska, and Kelly Ayotte of New Hampshire drafted an efficient, pragmatic deal they felt had a chance of passing on the floor. Two senators from the Democratic side of the aisle, Barbara A. Mikulski of Maryland and Patty Murray of Washington, quickly joined them. They worked long hours, compromised, and rallied votes behind them to solve the pressing problem directly related to the budget to prevent a government shutdown.

Their bipartisanship showed bravery. In an October 14, 2013 piece, *The New York Times* wrote that Collins "marched to the Senate floor and dared her colleagues to develop something better." Senator Ayotte gave a fiery address, which has been mythologized as the "reality-check speech," in which she told a floor of mostly men: "Where we find ourselves right now is unacceptable for America. It's unacceptable as leaders that the people of this country have elected. We owe it to our constituents to resolve this now."

Being brave means that you often face the consequences of your principles. "I probably will have retribution in my state," Murkowski said at the time. "That's fine. That doesn't bother me at all. If there is a backlash, hey, that's what goes on in DC, but in the meantime, there is a government that is shut down. Some people are hurting."[31]

These five women were by no means ideologically aligned. Kelly Ayotte could be classified as a Tea Party Republican. Barbara Mikulski first made waves by giving a controversial speech in 1970 at The Catholic University of America, in which she declared, "America is not a melting pot. It is a sizzling cauldron for the ethnic American who feels that he has been politically courted and legally extorted by both government and private enterprise."[32] Talk about a bridge to cross! Yet, these women could focus on the problem at hand and effectively find a solution.

Why could they get it done when no one else could? It's partly because they had a foundation of respect born out of their shared experiences overcoming gender barriers. They also spent time together and knew each other as politicians and as people. For years, the women of the Senate had been having bi-partisan pot-luck dinners. Every six weeks, they rotated hosting duties, welcoming each other into their homes. Each woman brought a dish, and they met each other's families. "I don't think it's a coincidence that women were so heavily involved in trying to end this stalemate," Ms. Collins told *The New York Times* shortly after the budget was passed. "Although we span the ideological spectrum, we are used to working together collaboratively."[33]

During the contentious election cycles that began in 2016, these dinners became a thing of the past. "The sisterhood has certainly faded," an unnamed insider source told Politico in 2020. That may seem like a small loss, given the massive problems this country faces, but I view it as significant. "Breaking bread" with our neighbors was an integral part of my upbringing in Montana. Interacting with people with whom you have personalized relationships builds respect, even with philosophical differences. I should know; I do this—break bread—with Ed all the time!

The idea of sitting down and hashing out differences with someone you respect but with whom you don't see eye-to-eye on many issues is a concept known as "deliberative democracy." In 2021, political scientists at Stanford and the University of Chicago examined the strategy's effectiveness through a study called "America in One Room," or "A1R." From September 19–22, 2019, they led a gathering of 500 voters in Dallas, Texas, in a nonpartisan discussion about the hot-button issues of the 2020 presidential election. These included immigration, health care, and climate change. "The participants were carefully selected to form an accurate, representative sample of the entire American electorate in all its political, cultural, and demographic diversity." As The Stanford Center for Deliberative Democracy's project website states, "Their views on the issues and the relative merits of the candidates will be documented and shared with the public, candidates, and policymakers, giving a clearer, more balanced, and more informed idea of the political landscape heading into the election."

The results of the study report that participants had become less polarized in their own views on government policy. Beyond that, they also reported feeling less negative toward people in the opposite party with opposing points of view.[34]

When we Americans talk to one another, making an effort to listen and absorb other perspectives, we are more likely to realize that we want the same things. We are more likely to compromise. We are more likely to solve problems. That's not a feel-good platitude; peer-reviewed data supports it. I'm a big believer in data. I should be. I've built a career out of using data to make my voice heard in rooms where it might have otherwise been ignored. That's why I was so glad to see Vice President Kamala Harris revive the female senator potlucks, which she did in June 2021. She invited all sitting female senators—sixteen Democrats and eight Republicans—to her residence for dinner. All but four attended. They talked about policy and compromise. Each brought a dish. The vice president made cheese puffs.

I know a few plates of cheese puffs aren't going to fix our schools or raise our wages. But when gathered together in good faith, these women have the power to make lasting change. Sometimes, starting simple, by breaking bread, can produce a solid foundation. I believe we can and will build on those foundations. I always bet on strong women.

Perhaps the potential of "deliberative democracy" can be seen when tackling significant issues, like student debt. In our polls, we've recognized a growing consensus for some form of student debt relief. Six in ten adults report struggling to make their student loan payments. Nearly two-thirds of Americans favor some level of debt forgiveness, and the majority support canceling all of it.[35] Yet those may only be short-term solutions. By listening and deliberating with Ed and colleagues on the other side of the aisle who see the issue through a different lens, I've been able also to view this issue from another angle. I've been able to consider their point of view respectfully and carefully.

I support canceling student debt, but this will not solve the root problem. A new generation will arrive, need degrees, and be saddled with more debt. To solve the problem, we must decrease the costs of attending college, limit student borrowing, and lower interest rates. Free or subsidized college tuition is another solution that can strike at the cause of the problem. Twenty states have implemented free community college programs. They are enormously successful and have pulled thousands out of poverty.

That's the *real* goal: economically advance people without saddling them with debts they cannot possibly hope to repay. No matter what your ideology, you can agree with that. Thus, we see each other more clearly when we deliberate, and a clearer vision can lead to more agreed-upon, bipartisan solutions.

Looking Ahead

In subsequent chapters, we'll examine the dangers of social and traditional media and how the COVID-19 epidemic is a perfect embodiment of our hyper-polarized state of affairs. We'll also suggest how the problem-solving strategies we discussed in this chapter can help resolve those issues. We have tools that can gradually lift us out of the sinking quicksand into which we now find ourselves. Our ability to make progress depends on whether we use them.

Chapter 6

Not So Social Media: Repairing a Once Promising Connectivity

Social media is a double-edged sword. On the one hand, it has opened up the democratic process to voices unheard in traditional media. No one can deny the positive impact when minority voices are included in dialogue on national issues. However, social media platforms also allow us to tap into our lesser selves—the parts of the human brain that respond to contention, controversy, and clicks. Social media has become a hotbed of misinformation and conspiracy theories. Driving the likes and views is a business model that employs algorithms designed to exploit human weaknesses and spawn outrage.

Outrage stimulates the same pleasure centers in the brain as hard drugs. Social media-related businesses exploit this vulnerability for profit. The challenge here is to reform social media while still allowing respectful, informed debate. This relatively new global technological connection, with its tentacles in just about every home and hearth and business on the planet, has, like any new thing, some severe growing pains to go through. That is no excuse for today's dysfunction and misuse rampant in online discourse. Democrats and Republicans agree on holding the platforms more accountable. Disinformation, fake news, and outright lies are infinitely repeated in ways that burn them into people's brains, altering reality with no regard for the actual objective facts in any given situation and often with dire consequences.

How We Got Here

It's easy to forget there was a time before all of us had our faces bent over tiny hand-held devices or stared at a desktop computer screen as it beams thousands of voices into our psyche. For Gen Z, kids born between 1997 and 2015, it's a different story than for older adults. They grew up with cell phones and computers and were the first generation never to know life *without* the internet. They were practically born with a cell phone, laptop, computer, or iPad in their hands. Today's youngsters, Gen Alpha, can't even imagine a life offline.

For Generation Z, social media is their first language. Online platforms, such as Facebook, Instagram, Snapchat, and YouTube, are productive forces in their lives and impact their understanding of how they should interact socially. Protections are needed that will allow them to navigate the internet safely. There is a growing body of empirical and anecdotal evidence that online interaction can increase mental health problems for teens, particularly girls ten to fourteen years old. Social arenas designed for youngsters must be optimized for social and emotional well-being in place of the for-profit model, which is currently designed in a way that fosters addiction and division.

The story of our current addiction to technology began in 1989 when British computer programmer Tim Berners-Lee, the acknowledged "father of the internet," went to his boss with an idea for an information management system, which his boss said was "vague but exciting."[36] That same year, America Online (AOL) became the online service. That era was called Gen Y, also known as millennials. They were babies born between 1980 and 1996. Given that LinkedIn was founded in 2002, Facebook in 2004, and Twitter was created in 2006, millennials, unlike Gen Z, didn't become fully immersed in internet use until they were older.

Fast forward to today, thirty years after he introduced his "vague but exciting" system, Tim Berners-Lee now runs an entity called the World Wide Web Consortium, which seeks to "establish clear norms, laws, and standards that underpin the webs." In this capacity, he has shared a warning about the "sources of dysfunction" the internet faces and how "the fight for the web is one of the most important causes of our time."[37] Berners-Lee's warning adds to a growing concern globally that powerful companies—controlling enormous amounts of user attention—put the prospect of open and fair internet discourse at risk.

Something the two of us share with Berners-Lee is his *optimism* about the future of the web. We agree with another statement he made, on a more positive note, when he said: "It would be defeatist and unimaginative to assume that the web as we know it can't be changed for the better in the next thirty [years]."[38]

How It Works

Digital technology is everywhere and continues to build, connecting us ever more closely. It has become *the* essential tool we use across all facets of society; its power and reach are immense. Unfortunately, technology's complexity and rate of innovation make it difficult for our laws to keep pace. Nowhere is this more so than in the sphere of social media—especially on such large socially and politically impactful platforms as Facebook and Twitter.

Internet businesses, massively technologic-based, know full well that the average user's attention span is short and the "hook" needs to go in right away. Thus, memes and social media apps are designed to cut out commentary and oversimplify complex issues. They deliberately play on the viewer's emotions, which is, in general, far more effective than appealing to reason.

Part of the challenge here is that most consumers don't understand how the system works. You go into your Facebook account for free. So how *do* they make money? It's simple: they generate revenue through your eyeballs, your *engagement*. The system was designed for engagement, with the metric determining the number of monthly active users, not for truth. That is what's at the core of the business model—the more eyeballs on their content, the better. To promote engagement, social media is designed to accentuate extremism. Studies from MIT show that disinformation on Twitter travels six times faster than the truth. This confirms an observation usually incorrectly attributed to Mark Twain that has since become a common maxim: "A lie can travel around the world before the truth has a chance to lace up its boots."

Social media can and does play a central role in people understanding one another. But from the *business* point of view, there is one overriding goal—to keep users on the platform. The longer you stay on Facebook or Twitter, the more ads you will see and the more money the companies make. This transition from social *networks* to social *media,* providing content beyond your social group, keeps you engaged and, thus, on the platform longer. Content that keeps people on the platform the longest is the most provocative and emotionally charged. It is also, ultimately, the most polarizing.

Social media amplifies the loudest and most polarizing voices like a global megaphone. The great irony is that most Americans—the centrists, the thinkers, and truth-seekers—are generally not heard.

Regrettably, tech giants have been unwilling to police themselves in ways they believe might adversely affect their bottom lines. Who *should* be responsible for shaping our tech future if we can't? We shouldn't just continue to allow tech companies free rein. What are the roles of the government, education, business, and the consumer? Leaders from all stakeholders' groups must come together to restructure the way things work and eliminate one of the most potent threats to our democracy.

Misinformation & Echo Chambers

It's no secret that anonymity reduces accountability. It's far easier to be disrespectful to someone online than when you are face-to-face. Social media also splinters the electorate into small, ideologically similar groups, segregated into "gated communities" of information—often *misinformation*. It is easy to find people who instantly reinforce your worldview. Candidates for public office can reach these constituencies directly, targeting their message to those specific groups.

People seek information that fits their current views, which ignores or discounts information contrary to their beliefs. This is called *confirmation bias*. Search engines and algorithms are happy to feed us a steady diet of information that supports what we already believe. As a result, we are becoming siloed, getting very little information contrary to our current perspectives. Deb Roy, a scientist and tenured professor at MIT, notes the original intent of the internet was to provide the technology for people to become more connected. "But what we've created in some ways is the ultimate self-sorting machine," he said during a video interview hosted by the JFK library and now on YouTube.[39]

Specific algorithms deliberately facilitate and accelerate the "othering" and demonization of competing viewpoints. Facebook's internal research admitted as much with this statement: "Our algorithms exploit the human brain's attraction to divisiveness."[40] Evidence shows that growing incivility on social media further polarizes its users and erodes trust. Without trust, there can be no respect. Without respect, we are stuck at a crossroads, unable to move forward in ways that will allow us to achieve our critical objectives as a society.

The willingness of extremists to create and spread complete fabrications has led to this cesspool of quicksand that threatens to pull us under. Arguments, claims, and positions no longer need to be grounded in *any* reality. Conspiracy theories that seem laughable to one side are believed with conviction by the other. There is so much misinformation, and it continues to get even more extreme. Misinformation and alternative facts are legitimized. Anyone with an agenda can go on TV or do a newspaper interview, complaining about "fake news." The morality of facts grounded in reality is discarded in favor of baseless untruths. Even when falsehoods are uncovered, they are often repeated so often that the truth is lost in the din.

The late Andrew James Breitbart was an American conservative journalist, writer, and commentator. After helping in the early stages of *Huffington Post* and the Drudge Report, he founded *Breitbart News,* a far-right news and opinion website. To Ed, *Breitbart News* was, in Ed's words, "the model for putting disinformation on a news website and using social media to trade it up the chain to gain an outsized amplified voice in our national conversations."

Over time, disinformation on *Breitbart News* has grown lucrative in businesses and politics. We have seen a progression in the power of disinformation campaigns that now mobilize groups to take concerted action—most notably in the January 6 Capitol Insurrection. The social media app Parler is currently the home base for alt-right, anti-vaxxers, conspiracy theorists, QAnon supporters, and other far-right extremists.

Misinformation is not benign. It impacts our elections, our pandemic and vaccination safety protocols, racial equality, and, above all, trust in our government and other institutions. Let's say it plainly: well-funded, well-organized, and sometimes even foreign operations all threaten civil political discourse, the integrity of our elections, and the overall well-being and future of our Republic.

Voters Weigh In

In our recent Battleground Polls, social media turned up front and center as a significant contributing factor to the lack of respect we now see everywhere. Those voters rightly felt that many social media users intentionally create division. They saw how many people feel safe holding their extreme positions and attacking others because they are behind a computer screen. The voters we polled were anxious about the social media platforms' algorithms that ensure people are only exposed to their current viewpoints. Here are some specific responses:

> *I think that social media plays a huge part in that as well. Because everybody's behind the screen, and they feel like they can say whatever they want without consequence.* (Independent Woman)

One of the things is[to] put the media with big tech,
break up big tech. They've got too much power, and
they control your speech. (Independent Senior)

Many voters voiced concerns about censorship, although this was an area of conflict for them because, at the same time, they were apprehensive about the amount of division and incivility they had seen on their feeds. Here are some more direct quotes:

I'm not saying we need to be censored, and people
need to tell us. Because it's a very touchy subject,
and I'm on the line with it. But we need some
type of oversight. (Independent Woman)

When we asked them about the concept of "de-platforming," voters had mixed reactions. There was strong support for freedom of speech, and at the same time, the respondents didn't believe people should be able to go on social media to instigate violence. Even among extreme conservatives, there was not much outrage that Trump was de-platformed from Twitter and Facebook.

The Biden group felt more strongly, as they viewed prohibition as a necessary response. Even those voters in the Biden group who were most concerned about censorship and our not losing freedom of speech felt that, in this particular case, the de-platforming *was* justified. As some remarked:

We have freedom of speech, and I feel like everyone
should be able to say what they want to say in regard to
topics or situations. However, for someone to go
on social media and instigate a situation that brings

about violence . . . that should not be tolerated.
(Independent Senior)

I'm torn on that because I do feel like you should have freedom of speech. I do—it's important to me, but I mean, I do feel like if you're inciting riots and like causing this huge chaos, there should be consequences.
(Independent Woman)

Interestingly, there was strong resistance to suggesting a hypothetical app that could provide you with opposing points of view. Participants rejected this idea because they believed this app would be flawed and that they could do a fine job of filtering out opposing views on their own.

Where We Go from Here

Dr. Joan Donovan, research director of the Harvard Kennedy School's Shorenstein Center on Media, Politics, and Public Policy, is an expert on online extremism, media manipulation, and disinformation campaigns. She draws parallels between the adverse effects of disinformation on social media and cigarette smoking and the tobacco industry. Large-scale misinformation, to her, is similar to secondhand smoke, in that it also degrades our public spaces and adversely affects the health of our democracy. And, as with Big Tobacco, only a few corporations benefit, while the vast majority of Americans pay the bill.

The tobacco industry fought long and hard against the regulation of cigarettes. They knew that once lawmakers understood the risks inherent in their products, legislation would be enacted that would be harmful to their corporate profit margins. In response to the mounting evidence that their products are harmful to the health of their users and those around them, the initial reaction from large technology companies has been similar to that of tobacco companies. As Dr. Donovan points out, Big Tobacco was forced to add warning labels on their packaging and advertisements. Likewise, Big Tech has put forth similar half-measures, such as filters and some supervision efforts on moderating content.

On the plus side of all this, we have seen positive changes. We are encouraged by feedback, with facts and not fake news, which shows us that most Americans *are* disturbed by disinformation and hate speech—and the degree to which they are allowed. Many people from all walks of life *have* spoken out against the vitriol. Nonetheless, it continues to be a complex and contentious issue, with some factions seeing the regulation of hate speech as in opposition to the first amendment's free speech protections.

Going back to the Parler example cited earlier, it became clear to both of us that Parler lacks substantive policies concerning hate speech. In a sure sign the industry needs national guidance, Parler agreed to filter hate speech posts on apps that Apple sells. However, we see them continuing to permit hate speech on Android and the internet overall.

Hate speech has led to violence, time and again, especially against minorities. The spike in Asian hate crimes associated with the pandemic has shaken the Asian community. Ninety-seven percent viewed violence against Asian-Americans as a serious issue in our polls. This view was found in all subgroups and three out of four respondents. Most people agree we should take legal action against hate speech and misinformation about Asian-Americans. Across party lines, people want the government to focus on the issue of anti-Asian hate crimes, which for many has roots in the finger-pointing of laboratories in Wuhan, China, as the root cause of the COVID-19 pandemic.

There is a clear need to restrict the tech model that uses algorithms to amplify extreme voices. Rather than limiting people's right to say what they believe, what we need to do to protect an individual's First Amendment rights *while* preventing harmful one-sided information from embedding itself into people's heads is to concentrate on getting the information out in the right way, showing all sides, and strengthening the data to be truthful and factual.

One way to promote more nuanced and inclusive discussions on social media is by expanding the number of buttons that allow for feedback. Facebook, for example, has added the following button reactions: love, care, ha-ha, wow, sad, and angry. Other sites have response buttons labeled Thought-Provoking, Caring and Warm-hearted, Helpful, Entertaining, Unfair, Uncivil, and Inappropriate. Adding an array of possible responses on Twitter would motivate people to post views outside their familiar choir, encouraging them to engage in more nuanced and complex discussions that acknowledge divergent views.

The simplicity of current "like vs. dislike" responses on Twitter and elsewhere ignores the complexity of important issues and ideas and inhibits critical thinking or discussion. Users base their reactions more on emotion than reason when they only choose to like or not like. They quickly judge what they've read rather than attempt to *understand* it. Interestingly, to address this, Twitter has added a feature when you retweet a news article; a prompt pops up asking if you want to actually read the article before retweeting it, as opposed to retweeting based on just the headline. Limited reaction choices discourage independent thought and lead to a group-think mentality, stifling alternative voices. A more extensive array of buttons would break the dichotomy of the like vs. dislike and us vs. them tribalism that drives much of the incivility, disrespect, and resultant mistrust in our now rampant national dialogue.

From our vantage point as pollsters, we see that people want technology to become more people-centered and less company-centered and for all users to have more choices and thus more control, which will help balance the power scale.

Though far from perfect, Wikipedia has been a successful model of a technology site run by a community of users rather than a corporate for-profit entity. Openly showing a user's goals for their being on a specific platform can also be a way to ensure that the correct information is presented to that individual. For instance, a person going on a platform to become *informed* about an issue would yield different results than someone who wants to be *entertained*. Sites can also be designed to give consumers more say in what kinds of responses they want available to them on particular sites, letting the company, organization, or other stakeholders know what they want to see.

There is incontrovertible evidence that women face more social media aggression than men. The demeaning and even hateful things people are willing to say about women candidates, and women of color, have significantly increased the negativity and division in our public discourse. On Twitter, female congressional candidates suffered about twice the abuse as males, and women of color fared even worse on Facebook and Twitter. On Twitter, Somali–American Democratic Congresswoman Ilhan Omar received the highest proportion of abusive messages of all candidates. On Facebook, Puerto Rican-American Democratic Congresswoman Alexandria Ocasio-Cortez ("AOC") received the highest proportion of abuse. Also on Facebook, Democratic women faced *ten times* the abusive comments of their male counterparts, while Republican women were twice as likely to have offensive comments posted about them. This is nothing less than systemic harassment of female public figures.

In the wake of the 2016 Russian interference debacle, the Big Tech companies have *started* to police themselves. But it's not enough. Fact-checking does not work. Typically, it reinforces the false claims because the other side mistrusts the fact-checker. Social media platforms, like Twitter and Facebook, will have to set and enforce fundamental standards. They can only be forums for agreement and civil conversations rather than the hot, unbound, uncivil maelstrom we see today. Many contend that if Big Tech companies, such as Facebook and Twitter, do not regulate themselves, the government may need to step in and do it for them.

Today, grassroots campaigns to reform media come from African American groups, organized labor, religious organizations, higher education, and other progressive organizations. These demands for reform focus on increasing the representation of different voices and urge political and media leaders to promote the democratization of the airwaves. They claim airwaves belong to the people, and the airwaves and news programs are being cheapened and sullied by commercial interests.

In 1996, Congress passed a "Communications Decency Act." Shockingly to us, a federal court declared it a violation of free speech rights, and the Supreme Court concurred. Thankfully, despite this Supreme Court decision, the Act's Section 230 remains in force today. Section 230 states, "No provider or user of an interactive computer service shall be treated as the publisher or speaker of any information provided by another information content provider."[41] Jeff Kosseff, an assistant professor of Cybersecurity Law at the United States Naval Academy, published a book in April 2019 titled *The Twenty-Six Words That Created the Internet,* based on the twenty-six-word sentence that comprises Section 230. Section 230 shields internet service providers and platforms, like Facebook and Twitter, from lawsuits stemming from user content. This has allowed for their rapid growth, along with the rapid growth of providers like YouTube, which would otherwise be required to check every one of the one hundred videos uploaded to their program every minute of every day.

There are no Section 230 type protections in the EU or Canada, so most popular social media platforms are based in the United States. Senator Chuck Grassley (R-IA) said, "It's time that we examine the need for Section 230 immunity and to what extent these tech companies are abusing their monopoly power."[42]

There are three main categories of remedies for improving Big Tech's current contentious social media mode. Foremost is *public safety.* Misuse of technology can be harmful to individuals and communities—especially communities of color—while compromising the integrity of the electoral process and our entire democracy. Reforming 230 to create liability for illegal content and reducing artificial amplification are meaningful goals to help ensure public safety. Nick Clegg, the vice president of Global Affairs for Facebook, has identified areas of bipartisan agreement in regulating social media platforms. First on his list is reforming Section 230.

We are aligned in our firm contention that large tech companies need to take responsibility and moderate content on their sites. They must implement clear, workable policies and practices to identify illegal content, hate speech, and misinformation. At the same time, Congress needs to create frameworks and regulations for the tech industry to follow. Having such legislation would begin a transparent process for reviewing social media content. Increased oversight and accountability will compel internet companies to follow best practices. With hate, extremism, and disinformation on social media platforms as toxic and destructive as wildfires, self-reporting and self-regulation by tech companies have so far failed. It is high time for the government to step in and regulate the social media industry—just as it regulates myriad industries that impact all citizens' safety and well-being, including food and health.

What is needed is a systems-based approach that moves beyond the current "whack-a-mole" approach of flagging individual harmful posts or illegal activity. Shining a light on the mechanisms used by social media platforms that harass, intimidate, and discriminate will guide us forward as we design strategies to mitigate the amplification of online extremism, abuse, and hate speech.

The second area in need of reform is *privacy and surveillance*. As noted earlier, Facebook and other platforms make money based on the eyeballs they bring to their content. Big Tech spies on us and profits by selling our attention to other entities that want to sell us something—be it an object or an idea. Reforms are needed to track and target self-interested surveillance and advertising practices. To protect consumer privacy, auditing and transparency systems are way past due.

Currently, one bill sits in the House called the "Information Privacy and Data Transparency Act" and another bill is in the Senate called the "Data Care Act." These pieces of legislation are designed to establish national standards that will protect the privacy and well-being of consumers. The bills would prohibit providers from using, disclosing, or selling any identifying data that could cause harm to the consumer. In addition, technology companies would be required to get opt-in approval from an appropriate government watchdog agency to sell private information. If such permission was granted, they would be required to keep records of when and to whom they share or sell our personal information.

Schools, medical institutions, lawyers, and financial institutions hold sensitive personal information and operate under consumer protection guidelines. Online platforms accumulate and retain the same type of private information, potentially harming the consumer. Yet they do not currently operate under any coordinated national rules and procedures. Legislators crafted our public policy under twentieth-century guidelines. Now, as we move ever more deeply into the Information Age, we must protect personal information from abuse by technology companies through carefully crafted twenty-first-century legislation.

The third area ripe for reform is *economical*. Big tech companies are monopolies that are crushing their competition. For instance, in 2020 alone, Apple's App Store brought in $64 billion. Apple charges a 30 percent fee for all apps downloaded from its app store and does not allow app makers to give their customers payment alternatives. App game maker Epic sued Apple for those allegedly monopolistic practices in Apple's app store. According to Epic's antitrust lawsuit, that deal amounts to a monopoly for a massively popular game, like Epic's Fortnite. When a federal judge issued his long-awaited ruling on this legal battle, neither side got what they wanted. Mark Lemley, a Stanford Law School professor and an expert on antitrust issues and technology, called the 180-page ruling a split decision. "It will improve competition on the edges, but it's not the fundamental change that Epic and advocates of the antitrust case would have hoped for," he said.[43]

The tech giants use their market dominance to bully or buy up competitors. Maintaining a free and fair market would reduce

Big Tech's market power. Antitrust legislation is an idea supported by both Republicans and Democrats. Senator Chuck Grassley, a Republican and president pro tempore emeritus of the Senate, and Amy Klobuchar (D-MN), have co-authored a bill that seeks to curb the market dominance of tech heavyweights. Senator Grassley spoke on the Senate floor against the power and monopolistic practices of the tech giants. He noted that Google controls 87 percent of the internet search market, Facebook has 2.8 billion monthly active users, people tweet 500 million times a day, and people watch over one billion hours of videos on YouTube every day. Senator Grassley said, "When a company has monopoly power, it no longer is constrained by normal market forces. If these platforms had competitors, consumers could choose alternatives. Right now, the only choice consumers have is to take it or leave it."[44]

This bill is part of a growing movement to educate consumers about the reliability—and most times unreliability—of news sources. Increased public media literacy makes sense. We can also educate children to be more critical thinkers whenever they consume information digitally. When online discussions are civil, they increase trust. Today's young adult users of this new technology hold the future in their hands. They need to step up and be the main driving force behind the reform efforts. We are doing everything *we* can to help encourage and facilitate that. This includes our participation in and promoting the civility programs for future political leaders held each year at Mo Elleithee's Georgetown Institute of Politics and Public Service. These programs serve as a launching pad for young leaders of tomorrow and are a prototype for other universities and institutions of higher learning to set up similar programs.

We are pollsters, not philosophers, but we have in common with philosophers that we also have to be keen observers of human behavior to be effective at our work. We must have a good idea of how people think and react in various circumstances. To that end, we do our best to keep up with literature and many aspects of popular culture. Sharing some of what we have delved into, we both learned a lot from the works of Joseph Campbell. In 1949, Campbell, a philosopher, teacher, and renowned author of classic comparative mythology books—*The Hero with a Thousand Faces* and *The Hero's Journey*—wrote about the duality of human nature and the shadow self.

Even before Campbell, in every one of his plays, from comedy to tragedy, Shakespeare's characters demonstrated the duality of human nature, showing that we all have different loyalties and flaws. The reality that we human beings are less than perfect is no surprise to anyone. Still, we urgently need to change our social media to help us be better and do better despite these human imperfections. We need to explore what's gone very wrong in our relationships with one another and, in that process, find ways to restore respect, trust, and basic human civility to our deeply divided nation.

Chapter 7

The News Media: Dousing the Flames of Discord

Ed's Respect Retreat

"**W**here are our Walter Cronkites?"

I posed this question to Celinda Lake and Mo Elleithee one evening in the summer of 2021 as we watched the sun go down from my porch in the low country of South Carolina. We had convened at my place for the better part of a week to hash through the political and social issues of the day and see if we could find some common ground—and perhaps some solutions. We nicknamed the trip, *The Respect Retreat.*

I followed up my question with an observation: "There are certainly no Cronkites on cable news."

"There are still some objective journalists out there," Mo responded. "They go on the local news at six at night for half an hour."

"And they don't get any eyeballs," said Celinda.

"The media class has a decision to make," I said, standing up to switch on a porch light.

"They've already decided," Celinda replied. "They are all about the bottom line."

"What I wouldn't give to hear Cronkite say, '*And that's the way it is*' one more time," I said.

Cronkite's signature line was more than a catchy sign-off for the nineteen years he hosted the CBS *Evening News*. It was a declaration of what a newscast should be: honest, unbiased, and based on fact. "Our job is only to hold up the mirror—to tell and show the public what has happened," Cronkite once said.[45]

That's a far cry from the current news landscape in 2022. That night in South Carolina, the three of us, who disagree on many matters of politics, agreed that something is fundamentally broken about our news media. It has grown increasingly uncivil, fueled by bias and competition for ratings, all of which degrade our public discourse. Media outlets promote stories for political ends; sensationalism triumphs over substance. Somewhere along the way, the truth has been discarded as irrelevant—or worse yet, boring.

As the dusk light faded to darkness, our conversation on the sorry state of the news media continued deep into the night. The question of blame was raised. While the condition of mainstream media reflects more significant societal issues, we decided the media class carries most of the burden of responsibility. We also discussed what share of the blame the media *consumers* bear, with differing opinions. In line with his position on other issues, Mo believed the public needed to take more responsibility for what they watched, read, and listened to. I thought the media and related institutions should hold themselves to a higher standard. Celinda landed somewhere in the middle.

Versions of this conversation are being had, right now, all across America on porches and across dinner tables. The tone of these conversations usually mirrors the same frustrated, nearly defeated attitude of my colleagues and me. But that night, the three of us, tired of constant lamentation, opened up a bottle of wine and, sitting across from each other, continued our discourse with a long and respectful conversation about what might be done about it. In this chapter, we'll offer some ideas we came up with.

As an aside, this conversation brought me back to my childhood dinner conversations, where we were encouraged to voice our opinions. I credit both of my parents for that great gift. Except when he was off to war, my father would be home every evening by 5:45, kiss my mother, and change out of his uniform. Then we would sit down as a family and watch the six o'clock evening news. When that was over at 6:30, we moved to the dinner table to eat and spend time talking about what we had just watched. Today, far fewer American families sit down together to have dinner, much less discuss the world's news around the dinner table. This, incidentally, was a tradition we kept when my father was away in Vietnam, a highly contentious time both about the war and racism. I also remember my father used to tell me, "The American Dream is really about the next generation, not only improving itself financially, but educationally, in their faith, and in their personal safety at home and abroad."

So in deconstructing what has gone so wrong with the media regarding the absence of fair and objective reporting, we also took an in-depth look at the broken parts of the American Dream.

The Current Landscape

Since platforms often shift, it is helpful to start this part of our examination by defining what we consider *traditional media*, especially since some are not "traditional." We sort traditional media into these three major categories:

1. Written journalism, which includes print and digital formats.
2. Broadcast news, both network and online shows.
3. Radio airwaves.

To fit the criteria, entities need to be explicitly concerned with news distribution, an admittedly broad spectrum. They also need to be working in tandem with media companies, not solely independent creators. For example, right-wing pundit Steven Crowder's massively popular YouTube show would qualify as traditional media because it's funded by The Blaze Media Corp, while leftist Glenn Greenwald's equally popular independent Substack newsletter would not. This broad definition leaves us with a veritable deluge of media from which to sift through, examine, and draw conclusions. Where, then, to begin? Well, with the people, of course.

Trust in news outlets is at an all-time low. Our 2021 Battleground Poll found that 60 percent of Americans trust only their local news outlet. ABC TV's level of national news trust is at 51 percent, and CNN is trusted by 47 percent of Americans. Voters reported feeling a lot of news fatigue. Participants in both groups admitted to being unable to keep watching or reading the news, feeling like they had to tune it out to prevent feeling overwhelmed and upset.

Our focus group participants also reflected distaste for the media. Here are some responses from a survey we conducted in June 2021:

I am just so frustrated. I don't know what to do anymore. I just turn off the news these days. That's why I don't bother anymore. (Independent Woman)

It's gotten to a point for me where I'm kind of over and done with all of it. I'm just kind of staying away from it because it's been a very rocky year looking at it all day, every day. (Independent Senior)

Voters did not blame any one person or institution, and many voters across both groups raised concerns about the role the media played in the division. However, even here, voters were split on which media outlets they blamed. Some Trump voters blamed the liberal media, while Biden voters seemed more concerned about all *cable* media. Although it wasn't a universal sentiment, almost all participants agreed the media has contributed to division and incivility in the country. When asked about *how* the media contributed to "incivility," voters had this to say:

It was a media problem. (Independent Senior)

Everything out there makes everybody polarized, and the media plays a big role in reinforcing that type of stuff too. (Independent Senior)

Trump voters largely blamed the Left, even wondering if the Left collaborated with the media to create further division in the country. Every voter in the Trump group agreed that the liberal media was a "big factor" in the divisions in our society.

Like everybody else is saying, they [the Left has] got newspapers, they got the media all on their side. So they can say pretty much whatever they want. (Independent Senior)

This woman's sentiment is heartfelt, but it doesn't tell the whole story. Yes, there are plenty of liberal newspapers, but there is no shortage of "the other side" out there for every ideological mindset. News outlets that promote a single ideology have always existed, and they always will. One can look back to a 1789 newspaper, *The Gazette of The United States,* which supported The Federalist Party, rivalry with the *National Gazette* and the *Philadelphia Aurora* newspapers, which were for the Democratic-Republicans. The mud-slinging in print that went on back then was just as ferocious as today and no less partisan. If we search through the annals of our country's relationship with the press, this pattern has continued to repeat itself. The policies they argue over continue to change, but the divide remains partisan.

Given this history, we're not here to critique the political messages of media outlets but want to examine the modern mechanisms through which they are delivered. It is hard to convince Americans that the positions they are consuming are biased when they have been steeped in that messaging for decades. Telling a long-time FOX News or MSNBC viewer that their pundits are blinded by ideology usually elicits this kind of response: "Well, the other side does it too, and they are far worse!" We hope that if we can trace some similarities in *how* those messages are delivered, we can show how the same techniques are used to divide us on both ends of the spectrum. Those mechanisms are unique to this era and are uniquely dangerous.

This chapter will look at five primary ways the news is delivered—ways that divide Americans and foster a lack of respect in our national dialogue.

1. Outlets use negativity to generate clicks and eyeballs, which translates to dollars.

2. Information "silos" keep viewers and readers glued to a particular ideology, preventing respectful disagreement and dialogue.
3. Pundits and publications cater to the cynical voter.
4. Media outlets now define the news rather than report it.
5. The media uses non-issues, such as political correctness, to drum up outrage rather than focusing on root issues.

We will delve into each of these factors in detail in the coming pages. The best place to start is with the question Ed posed at the outset: *Where are our Walter Cronkites?* To tell the story of how our current media landscape ended up where it is now, we need to examine the history of cable news, how it morphed into toxicity, and what we can do to inject the spirit of respect back into the discourse.

Cable News

Cable news has become a toxic, polarizing format. That's true—and, as we said before, it's not unique to this age. Before the "golden era" of cable news, ushered in by Cronkite and his fellows in the 1960s, there was no such thing as non-partisan media. Information was controlled by the political leanings of those who owned the newspaper. Oklahoma billionaire businessman Edward Gaylord owned *The Oklahoman* newspaper, and, no surprise, they ran his right-wing editorials on the front page of the paper. Hardly unbiased reporting. There was a newspaper for every perspective. In the 1940s, New York City had *seven* different daily newspapers, and you knew what someone's politics were by which newspaper they bought.

At the beginning of the electronic age, things changed with the advent of long-form news radio and with the three major news networks: CBS, NBC, and ABC. There was a blip of time in our history when our media was a little bit less partisan. TV networks decided to use a business model that focused on facts over bluster to their great credit. The prevailing sentiment was: "Walter Cronkite is going to lay the facts out for you. You go from there."

Then people figured out how to make radio and television feel more like the newspapers of old and have a partisan bend. This change started with talk radio and moved to cable news. Our media ecosystem, which rightfully feels terrible and *is* terrible, is, in fact, where it has been most of the time. It's just at scale, with broadcasts adding a whole new dimension to the toxicity.

In the Cronkite era, news organizations reported more broadly on events and weren't playing to such specific audiences. They wanted their news reports to appeal to *all* Americans, regardless of political affiliations. Respect for the truth and impartiality were the foundations upon which the networks reported the news. Cronkite said, "In seeking truth, you have to get both sides of a story."

In the current echo chamber of modern mass media, people only hear one side of any story. Today, watching the same event or piece of legislation variously covered by FOX and CNN can be entertaining and concerning. Neither will flip the coin over to balance their reporting. They view their partisanship as a necessary counterweight to the bias of their competition. Americans selectively watch FOX, CNN, or MSNBC, which is *all* they watch. We choose the information, be it newspapers, magazines, talk shows, or other outlets that support our worldview, disregarding contradictory facts. They feel comforted in continuously validating their beliefs via the twenty-four-hour news cycle.

Whatever your political bias, you have an assortment of outlets that will affirm your ideology. Angry at Biden? See your rage reflected by your favorite anchor and panel of experts. Have you lost your job to economic forces beyond your control? Turn on the TV and let your news outlet hand you a scapegoat.

Over time, tools have been developed to manipulate cynical voters. Cable news has found the "information silos" that we mentioned before particularly useful. The term comes from the business world. There, the term refers to independent divisions that don't share their information. Silos function much the same way in the news media: communication nose-dives, factions form, and productivity decreases. When it comes to cable news, the issue is that this business model *works* for the network but not for the consumer. Media outlets discovered that if they took hardcore positions as a silo for people to "stay in," they solidified and increased their audience.

This massive issue runs deeper than politics. When people watch cable news, they aren't getting information that only informs how they view the political class. Their viewing silo becomes how they view *America* and how they view *society*. It influences how they view *the world*. The networks have adopted their worldviews as a "home base" for people who share those views.

Data from our Battleground Poll bears this out to an alarming degree—across all hot-button issues of the day. Black Lives Matter's favorable/unfavorable rating among FOX News viewers is 17/78. Among non-FOX viewers, it's 59/35. QAnon has a 27 percent unfavorable rating among FOX viewers, with 44 percent having never heard of it. Among non-FOX viewers, it has a 57 percent negative rating, with only 30 percent having never heard of it.

Dr. Anthony Fauci has a favorable/unfavorable rating among daily FOX viewers of 20 percent favorable to 69 percent unfavorable, while among non-FOX viewers, it's 64 percent favorable and

27 percent unfavorable. Fifty-six percent of daily FOX viewers cite "cancel culture" as an extremely or very fundamental problem, compared to only 32 percent of non-viewers. There is one notable exception: majorities of both daily FOX viewers (56 percent) and non-viewers (69 percent) say that refusing to accept election results is an extremely important or very important problem.

These echo chambers are a big problem, one that is compounded by other techniques the cable news networks use to divide the electorate. One of those techniques is how they change the framework of stories. Instead of reporting the news, as Cronkite did, media outlets now *define* it. FOX has been at the vanguard of a significant change in how information is presented. FOX successfully drove the negative campaigns against the Green New Deal and Medicare for All by defining those issues for their viewers. They're covering news how they know their audience will react to it.

In his 2013 book *Informing the News,* Harvard professor Thomas Patterson argues that cable news networks have developed an easy, inexpensive, and ingenious strategy. When a politician does something newsworthy, journalists reach out to opponents or experts who they know will attack that position. The crucial component of this aggressive approach is not the more time-consuming and challenging task of a careful investigation of the facts but rather a relatively easy quest to find someone to "rip things apart." Cable news shows often assemble a *panel* of experts and politicians on both sides of the spectrum that attack a story's originator while also attacking the other panel members.

Our toxic incentive structure directly feeds into this model. Celinda knows many reporters who write perfectly decent, well-balanced articles for the *Washington Post.* Still, when they go on cable news, they become polarizing talking heads. Why? Their Twitter follower count jumps up whenever they have a particularly vitriolic segment. That's how they get rewarded. Sponsors love social media metrics.

In their efforts to attract more viewers, cable news caters to the cynical voter. Ed believes Tucker Carlson was once a very thoughtful, reasonable conservative—one of the best reporters, who always did his research and came up with good, fact-based questions. Then FOX gave him an evening show, where he took over for Bill O'Reilly, and suddenly, to Ed's astonishment, he became a demagogue. His rhetoric exploits viewers by appealing to their fears and prejudices for political purposes. To Ed, Sean Hannity is another prime example of this new breed of entertainment journalists. Ed describes Hannity's style as bombastic and says he often sounds like Macbeth's line about life being "a tale told by an idiot, full of sound and fury, signifying nothing."

In the end, it's all about eyeballs. The market drives coverage. It's caused by the sponsors, the donors, and the viewers.

That night in South Carolina, Mo told a story about traveling through Europe in 2016. He turned on CNN International, and there was wall-to-wall coverage of the Battle of Aleppo—a big story in Syria at the time and a conflict sometimes referred to as "Syria's Stalingrad." The next day, he flew home and turned on CNN. To his surprise, there was no mention of Aleppo—not because it was any less newsworthy, but because it's not what the American audiences cared about. Instead, he found the usual talking heads arguing over some issue that has now faded away, long forgotten, yet the people of Aleppo are still suffering.

Aleppo was unquestionably an important story that certainly merited more coverage here. But a lack of journalistic integrity prevented the story from being reported because the bottom line would have been impacted, which is a short-sided point of view. Until we find a way to reject this bottom line, important stories will be ignored while our national dialogue continues to degrade.

Lack of Journalistic Rigor

Cable news, to us, is undoubtedly the most egregious example of the most egregious actors, especially on the prime-time shows in the evening on all three cable news networks. But polarization amongst the *rest* of the media is no less stark. AM Radio ranks with pundits who seem to be frothing at the mouth as they blast vitriol across the airwaves, creating their own "silos." Media scholar and Tufts professor Jeffrey Berry, who co-authored an exhaustive examination of the political-cum-media landscape in 2014's *The Outrage Industry,* says the way conservative radio hits back against the mainstream media is almost self-reinforcing. "It's an obvious business model," he says. "Tell your audience that the mainstream media is corrupt and biased, then there's all the more reason to turn to your conservative talk radio to get the truth."[46]

On the other side of the spectrum, conservatives don't trust the *Washington Post* or the *New York Times.* They see them as putting their thumb on the scale. Conservatives generally perceive both influential daily newspapers as left-leaning. But they have more significant problems than their political bias. We want to stress here that factors like our toxic incentive model and "click"-driven journalism hurt the quality of the written word *more* than partisanship. Let's look at how that functions.

News organizations now judge individual media outlets by their Twitter and Instagram following rather than their journalistic accomplishments. This evaluation method leads to more division and more incivility because journalists fully understand the power of negativity. Almost everyone will tell you they don't like nega-tivity, yet they respond to it. Ironically, young college women say they least prefer negative advertising, yet in all the studies, they are the most strongly influenced by it.

We know humans remember the negative more than we do the positive. A recent study found that fans of sports teams recall their team's losses more than their wins. Negativity has a *stickiness* to it that remains with the consumer. The two most potent ways to mobilize people are to stimulate their anger and loss aversion. Both of these negative emotions feed division and incivility. The sophis-tication of our campaigns, social media platforms, and cable news has accelerated the trend toward negativity.

Like cable news, traditional newspapers have changed how they report the information. Journalists now put their own words at the story's center and weave the news into their narrative to become secondary to style. Local newspapers have traditionally focused more on facts than on ideology and have been a more trusted source of unbiased news for many Americans. Alarmingly, 25 percent of all local newspapers have gone belly-up in the last fifteen years.

Additionally, the transition from print to online content has been fraught with ethical choices for newspapers. "Clickbait"—especially in the form of those sensationalized headlines—gets attention but ultimately erodes consumer confidence in what they're seeing. Nonetheless, they deliver those all-important eye-balls and, therefore, drive news corporation profits. In an era where the written word is competing against television, social media, and the internet, newspapers are caught between the reality of econom-ics and the time-tested values of responsible journalism.

In 2019, Temple University published an exhaustive study titled, "Aggregation, Clickbait and Their Effect on Perceptions of Journalistic Credibility and Quality." In the study, co-authors Logan Molyneux and Mark Coddington, both professors of journalism, wrote, "In the late 2000s and early 2010s, the commercial pressures to pile up page views to feed a digital advertising-based business model pushed more news organizations to rely on aggregation themselves. The same traffic-based economic model has also fed the rise of dubious methods of attracting attention to hastily produced online material. Most notably, 'clickbait' has emerged as a widely used term to deride and dismiss content that exists more as a way to lure audiences to click on it—inevitably letting those audiences down—than for any informative purpose. On the other hand, clickbait headlines appear to have a broadly negative impact on audience perceptions. Results also suggest clickbait headlines may lower perceptions of credibility and quality."[47]

There's no getting around the fact that clickbait, sound bites, and headlines have consequences in the real world. A January 2016 study by the University of Texas at Austin's Center for Media Engagement found that emotionally charged headlines can change perceptions of a criminal suspect's supposed guilt, influence how individuals assess political candidates, and affect comprehension and memory of news articles.[48]

A free press plays a vital role in any representative government. Democracy thrives when its citizenry is well-informed. Incivility in the media, continuously reinforced by twenty-four hours of news programming, becomes a vicious cycle. How the press behaves means they bear some responsibility for the breakdown in trust and respect in our society. Media outlets certainly need to do a better job of policing themselves. News organizations need to decide if they are here to inform the public. However, as Celinda stated that night on Ed's porch, "They are here for the bottom line."

An Over-Emphasis on Political Correctness

Celinda here. One of the tenets of the respectful relationship between Ed and me is that we listen, we learn, and even when we differ, we respect others' opinions and want to understand them. With that in mind, I want to end this chapter with a quick coda on what Ed believes about the media and how he sees it as incivility outrage by over-focusing on political correctness rather than focusing on real issues.

Ed is far from a reactionary who wants things to go back to "the good old days," but his concern is that root issues are being ignored while seeking a purity that does not exist in our entertainers, politicians, and public people. He says that it's much easier to go after a comedian who says the "wrong" thing on stage than it is to fix, say, the water crisis in Flint. He believes we are offering up sacrificial lambs to the altar of perfection instead of rolling up our sleeves and getting to work on the problems that affect Americans.

Ed believes the media knows this and exploits it. I can't disagree when he says, "A simple Google search will return headline after headline picking apart the most benign of statements. People lose careers over a slip of the tongue. The media whips people up into a frenzy that feeds on itself. To my mind, Walter Cronkite wouldn't have given the time of day to a pop star saying 'the wrong thing' at a concert when there were so many more pressing issues at hand. He would have reported on inflation, on jobs, on the crisis in the Middle East."

Ed told me many times that these views don't represent the majority of Americans. Our Battleground Polls show that over two-thirds of Americans don't fit into solid ideological camps—the type of camps that champion ideas like strict political correctness. A bevy of research backs up that data. In October 2018, scholars Stephen Hawkins, Daniel Yudkin, Miriam Juan-Torres, and Tim Dixon published a report through the nonprofit More in Common called "Hidden Tribes: A Study of America's Polarized Landscape." That report argued that most voters fall into the "exhausted majority." Their members share a sense of fatigue with our polarized national conversation, a willingness to be flexible in their political viewpoints, and a lack of voice in the national conversation. "They also dislike political correctness. Among the general population, a full eighty percent believe that 'political correctness is a problem in our country," the authors write. "Even young people are uncomfortable with it, including seventy-four percent of voters 24 to 29, and seventy-nine percent of voters under age 24."[49]

Ed believes one of the most significant impacts of political correctness is our youth. They are being taught there is only one way to see things, one way to think, which is contrary to and dampens learning "critical thinking" based on exploring all of the objective analyses and evaluations of an issue to form a judgment.

Ed's conviction is firm, and he sees it backed up by data that most Americans want to move on from this period of culture wars. He maintains we don't want to be at each other's throats, yet the media we absorb constantly encourages us to hold each other to standards that nobody can live up to. Ed reports that actor and author Stephen Fry put it very well to an audience of thousands when he said, during the 2018 Munk Debates, where the topic was political correctness, "The two sides of the cultural war, which are no longer left and right, they're something deeper and weirder and odder, are drifting further and further apart every week that passes. Such that each is standing on its edge, yelling at the other, and neither is hearing. They're just making frantic faces at each other." To thunderous applause, he added, "It's a terrible shame to live in this culture and feel there's so much hostility, resentment. We've seen what happens when it goes to extremes; we've seen the terrible carnage and destruction that can cause."[50]

Ed doesn't want America to continue to head toward those extremes. Neither do I. Ed believes we need to ignore the negative or sensationalized messaging by the media, no matter how tantalizing it is, no matter how much it activates our base impulses, and get back to listening to one another. If we can do that, we might replace the resentment we don't even *really* feel with a new respect for one another.

Chapter 8

Reforms: Tackling Campaign Finance Regulation and Special Interest Privilege

Money has always been inseparable from politics. To some extent, it always will be. In how they compete, powerful entities further their interests by donating to campaigns and putting dollars behind causes. That's the reality of the situation.

We deal in reality, not with an imagined utopia that does not factor in human behavior—much of which we learned in the trenches as pollsters. Indeed, the premise of this book is a frank and pragmatic dialogue between two colleagues. By openly acknowledging and discussing truths that not everyone likes to admit, first with each other and now with you, we can begin to think about how the mechanisms that drive some of these practices might be reformed.

That money is inseparable from politics doesn't mean the way it's currently injected into campaigns—without transparency and in record amounts—is functional, acceptable, or positive. Special interests wield far too much influence. Super PACs give enormous privileges to mega-donors and corporations, unions, and advocacy groups with deep pockets and take control of most of the campaign spending and messages out of control of the actual candidate and their campaigns.

Simply put, America's campaign finance system is broken. Dark money, funds from groups that do not disclose their donors, has become a driving political force, estimated to be more than a billion dollars in the 2020 federal campaigns. Additionally, the problem with this current independent spending is not a factor that benefits Republicans over Democrats in their campaigns. Analysis of the "dark money" spending showed slightly more than half ($514 million) of the 2020 spending went to help Democrats, and $174 million was put behind the Biden candidacy.

Data illuminates how rampant the problem has become. According to The Brennan Center for Justice, a nonprofit, since 2010, powerful groups have poured more than $1 billion into federal elections. It's an issue not just on the national level; state elections are frequently swayed by large injections of untraceable dark money. Chris Herstam, a former Republican majority whip in the Arizona House of Representatives and now lobbyist, told The Brennan Center, "In my thirty-three years in Arizona politics and government, dark money is the most corrupting influence I have seen."[51]

Our current campaign finance laws allow this system to perpetuate itself, even though most Americans see these laws as flawed and inadequate. Republican and Democratic voters believe we should prioritize campaign finance reform. According to our Battleground Poll, more than 80 percent of voters from both political parties want *greater transparency* for campaign contributions. That desire for systemic change exists. And we both have some ideas on how that change might take hold. However, before we tell you our beliefs, it may prove helpful to shine a light on the recent history of how money functions in the political sphere. Examining how we got to the position we're in might give us insights into how we can maneuver out of it.

How We Got Here

The primary responsibility of the legislative branch is to create laws, not raise money. But in the late 1990s, there was a change in the culture of Washington politics. Before that time, representatives typically spent eighteen months legislating in Washington and six months campaigning for reelection. Then, about thirty years ago, congressional representatives began to spend less time legislating and more time fundraising. Now, they must fundraise from the moment they are elected; supporters of victorious candidates often receive fundraising requests the same evening their candidate is elected.

The time required to fundraise has adverse effects on Congress's ability to govern effectively. Members of the House and Senate typically spend two to four hours a day on fundraising calls or attending campaign fundraisers in the evenings. All of the time and energy spent raising money detracts from Congress's ability to govern. There is simply not enough time to do the business of the people *and* the business of the campaign. As a result, Congress has become increasingly less productive and less functional.

In the current political process, soliciting money from large donors potentially amplifies and distorts the voice of wealthy donors. More importantly, major donors often have different priorities from the average voters. Congress usually spends an excessive amount of time on legislation important to their donors and less time on matters that improve the lives of their constituents. Representatives are often advised to "lean to the green," a reference to backing legislation favored by the people who will bankroll your reelection. This is not illegal but, from an ethical point of view, can certainly be seen as a systemic corruption of representative democracy . . . rightly further adding to voter cynicism.

The endless cycle of fundraising has a chilling impact on civility and respect. Effective fundraising today requires candidates to arouse animosity and distrust of the other side. Negative campaigning generates more money than speaking about the issues. Firing up the base leads to incivility and makes goodwill and compromise across the aisle more difficult.

Time constraints of modern fundraising certainly play their part. However, no discussion of this issue would be complete without considering the 2010 Supreme Court case, *Citizens United v. Federal Election Commission.* The 5–4 landmark decision barred the government from interfering with an individual's or corporation's right to free speech. The majority decision, written by Justice Anthony Kennedy, stated, "If the First Amendment has any force, it prohibits Congress from fining or jailing citizens, or associates of citizens, for simply engaging in political speech. Free speech in today's America costs money, i.e., advertising, and any restriction on money is, therefore, a restriction on free speech."[52]

Justice John Stevens wrote the dissenting opinion. Stevens postulated, "The Court's ruling threatens to undermine the integrity of elected institutions across the nation." The four dissenting justices wrote that the majority failed to consider the detrimental effects of even the appearance of corruption by unfettered corporate money.

Justice Stevens argued that corporations were dangerous to democracy because of their loyalty to profit, not country. Corporations can raise enormous sums of money that affect how people vote. The legislative branch needs to regulate its influence on the democratic process.

Citizens United opened the floodgates, and dollars came flooding into our elections. All of a sudden, independent entities could spend *millions* on races, effectively taking the place of political parties and campaigns in terms of importance. A 2020 report by Open Secrets, a nonprofit that follows money in politics, details the impact of the decision. As Sheila Krumholz, executive director of the Center for Responsive Politics, stated, "In our 35 years of following the money, we've never seen a court decision transform the campaign finance system as drastically as Citizens United. We have a decade of evidence, demonstrated by nearly one billion dark money dollars that the Supreme Court got it wrong when they said political spending from independent groups would be coupled with necessary disclosure."[53]

The decision was a watershed moment in campaign finance; it allowed corporations and unions to spend unlimited amounts of money and gave rise to the proliferation of Super PACs. A Super PAC is designed to influence a specific election. Super PACs function independently from any candidate or political party. Individuals, corporations, unions, and other political action committees (PACs) may make unlimited contributions to a Super PAC. There is no cap. Contributions are non-reportable. Decreased transparency means less accountability. Super-PACs can spend endless amounts of money on the cause or candidate they support. Again, according to The Center for Responsive Politics, Super-PACs raised over $3.3 billion in the 2020 election cycle. That is nearly double the $1.8 billion raised during the 2016 presidential election cycle.[54]

Critics argue that this deluge of corporate, union, and advocacy group money drowned out the voices of ordinary Americans. Those relatively few donors who contribute more than $100,000 dominate the total funding from the millions of small donors contributing to political campaigns. Although the overall number of small donors has increased, their share of total donations has remained a steady 20 percent. A select few billionaires and millionaires have had an outsized influence on our democracy by funding Super-PACs.

The Supreme Court justices who were the majority vote may have mistakenly believed that Super PACs, like the court case Citizens United, would play a minor role in campaigns simply because they were prohibited from coordinating with candidates.

Voters see campaign finance as an area that needs to be addressed across the political spectrum, and this is an area where our political prescriptions are significantly different. Rather than view this as a barrier to respectful dialogue, we've taken the time to see *why* each of us thinks the way we do. And while the methods by which we each want to bring about change differ, our goal is the same: to reform our campaign finance system to create a transparent process that serves the needs of both the public and those wanting to serve the public through political office.

Ed on Squeezing the Balloon of Campaign Finance

Celinda has a democratic approach to campaign finance reform: using legislation to require smaller contributions and limit enormous contributions. No matter how you change the rules, people will find a way around those rules to funnel money into the system. They always have, and they always will. That may seem cynical, but if you know anything about me, I'm the furthest thing from a cynic. I'm just a realist about this particular aspect of human nature. To me, pretty much all of recorded history backs up my position. Think of money in politics as like air in a giant balloon. If you squeeze the balloon on one end, it will just expand on the other end. The amount of air doesn't change. The Supreme Court decision in Citizens United affirmed that people have a Constitutional right to voice their opinion, and they can do that through a contribution. I don't foresee a Constitutional Amendment overturning that decision.

But something needs to change. In addition to polling, I've been on the strategic team of several political campaigns and seen first-hand how, since the "dawn of the Super PAC," candidates have far less control over their own messaging. In today's political arena, a campaign is lucky if between the "pro" Super PACs, "anti" Super PACs, and the opponent's campaign, they control 25 percent of the campaign's messages, often less. So a campaign's strategy team on both sides is put at a disadvantage. First and foremost, the "anti" Super PACs often assume the role of initiating the attack. There have even been situations where our campaign wanted to run a positive message, and the "pro" Super PAC decided we were not doing the right thing. They initiated the attack on our opponent, contradicting our campaign's critical strategic talking point about wanting to run a positive campaign.

Is campaign finance reform the answer? I don't think so. Especially if all you are doing is squeezing one end of the balloon and expecting it to take some of the air (i.e., money) out of the system. Politicians who, in trying to be responsive to perceived corruption from significant contributions, put significant restrictions on campaign contributions in the last go-around of campaign finance reform; however, they squeezed the balloon at one end, only to see it expand at the other end with Super PACs. It opened up loop-holes they didn't see coming, allowing unaccountable dark money to stream into campaigns, which fueled further distrust.

One of the unintended consequences of these attempts at campaign finance reform was that it took "soft money" away from the two political parties. The rise of Super PACs weakened both political parties as the flow of money moved away from the center and farther to the extreme left and right. I can't tell you the number of campaign managers I know who hate Super PACs, which are supposed to be "helping" them but have only resulted in the loss of control of their messages.

My answer is not to minimize, but rather maximize the money that can go into the campaign's direct control. Let's take off the limits on contributions made directly to campaigns and make it such that donations are instantly and thoroughly reported so you have transparency. It will put the control back into the campaigns. Additionally, that will eliminate this "wink, wink, nod, nod; I'll do your dirty work" approach of Super PACs that has only put the increasingly aggressive approach of today's campaigns in the forefront. This approach was recently implemented through new campaign finance laws in Virginia. In the recent gubernatorial election, most of the money going to Super PACs went directly into the campaigns. The air in the balloon did not get any less, but it shifted those monies more directly under the control of the campaign.

As another bonus, this system would allow donors to pressure the campaigns to play to the positive instead of the negative. Republicans need to be for something; we can't just pontificate about what we're against. Until our campaigns get to a point where they control a majority of messages, they will not effectively "accentuate the positive" and show workable solutions to our most pressing problems. Because the Super PACs drive the negative campaigns, more control of the message by the campaigns means they can drive the positive messages and, if they go too negative, be held responsible for that style of campaigning.

Celinda Weighs in on Why She Favors Reform

Ed and I fully agree that Super PACs should have less power. The average Senate race has more than 60 percent of its ad messages delivered by somebody else. That's appalling. If you're going to run for something and put yourself on the line, you ought to be in control of your message.

Ed's solutions would do it by allowing unlimited campaign finance from any donors directly to the campaigns. My solution is different: I want public financing of campaigns. Why should I give a billionaire more access than me? I don't believe in that. I support passing a Constitutional Amendment to overturn the Citizens United decision. Ed and I want the same result. We don't have to agree on the solution and can still respect each other's thinking.

Barring a Constitutional Amendment, we still, in my opinion, need to pass legislation that moves the needle. One step in the right direction was 2019's For the People Act, which attempted to rectify the problems caused by Super PACs and amplify the voices of ordinary Americans in a democratic process. Under the bill's provisions, candidates for the US House of Representatives and presidential hopefuls would be eligible to receive public money to fund their campaigns. Individual small-donor contributions of up to $200 would be matched six to one. All money would be paid from the Freedom From Influence Fund. A surcharge on civil and criminal judgments against corporations would be the main source of its funding and would not require any taxpayer money. Participation would be voluntary and require candidates to adhere to rules and restrictions, including spending less than $50,000 of their own money and limiting campaign contributions to $1,000 or less. Recipients would be obligated to disclose all campaign contributors.

I can tell you that this idea is hardly new. President Theodore Roosevelt proposed the nascent concept in his 1907 State of the Union address. Roosevelt said, "The need for collecting large campaign funds would vanish if Congress provided an appropriation for the proper and legitimate expenses of each of the great national parties,"[55] an appropriation ample enough to meet the necessity for thorough organization and machinery, which requires a large expenditure of money. Then the stipulation should be made that no party receiving campaign funds from the Treasury should accept more than a fixed amount from any individual subscriber or donor.

The small-donor model has been tested at the local level with impressive results. In New York City, 90 percent of candidates in the primaries participate in the publicly funded program. The matching funds program has helped more minority candidates run for office. David Dinkins, the city's first Black mayor, was an early participant. Small donor contributions and community engagement have increased. Races have been more competitive, and incumbents have enjoyed less advantage against challengers. Candidates have been more responsive to the needs of their constituency because they know they will run in competitive elections. Special interest money accounts for only 6 percent of all contributions.

The For the People Act sought to correct the current imbalance between Super PACs and traditional political party spending regulations. Super PACs are subject to less regulation and spending limits than political parties. This legislation would permit political parties to establish small donor funds to double the money they can give to candidates.

Critics of the current campaign finance laws point to good intentions that spawned unintended consequences. Decreased reliance on political party money has been a factor in the rise of Super PACs and dark money. Super PACs move issues more toward the extremes, which hinders compromise toward a middle ground. Political parties are often moderating factors in elections because they are accountable to larger bases and speak for a more diverse and moderate constituency. Sadly, The For the People Act stalled in passing the Senate, but I think there can be other legislation introduced that achieves similar goals.

One good way of getting more small donors involved in the political process is through voucher programs. For example, Seattle's democracy voucher program has successfully increased participation in the political process by ordinary citizens. Twenty thousand Seattle small donors, including people from traditionally underrepresented groups, contributed $1.14 million to political candidates in 2017. In elections where democracy vouchers were given to Seattle voters, the number of donors who lived outside Seattle decreased. This program has reduced the influence of big-money donors and corporations and made candidates and office-holders more responsive to the needs of the people they serve.

The cost of providing vouchers for federal elections on a national level is estimated at between $3 billion and $6 billion a year. While this figure sounds enormous, it is a drop in the bucket compared to the estimated $100 billion in corporate tax breaks, grants, and other unfairly advantageous monetary policies to select entities. If federal officeholders are no longer beholden to large corporations, they would no longer be incentivized to pass sweetheart deals for major corporate donors. Reducing the cost of corporate welfare by even 6 percent would pay for the voucher program. Representatives would spend their fundraising time at community-based events, fundraising from voucher holders. This dynamic would create more contact between candidates and average citizens.

Currently, there are fourteen states with some form of public financing option for state-wide elections. They have similar rules that candidates must follow to qualify for public funds. For example, in Hawaii, candidates who opted into the program were awarded funds similar to amounts raised by their competitors. Interestingly, in the 2014 Arizona gubernatorial election, privately funded candidates spent twice as much as their publicly funded opponents.

The current presidential election financing program matches donations at a one-to-one ratio for presidential primaries. Candidates polling at 5 percent or more are eligible for block grants for the general election: $103.7 million in 2020. The legislation I propose we should institute would increase the amount of money political parties can use to support their candidates. Ronald Reagan participated in the presidential election financing program and was elected by a landslide in 1980 without holding a single fundraising event. Times have certainly changed, and since 2012, no major presidential nominee has ever again used the system.

Interference by foreign entities is also an issue. These governments have attempted to influence our elections through dark money and campaign ads. Provisions in the legislation would prohibit targeted online political ads paid for by other countries in an attempt to influence our elections. In 2016, Russian operatives linked to the Kremlin produced and bought time to air thousands of social media ads meant to increase social discord, suppress minority votes, and impact the election. These ads targeted battleground states and reached over 127 million Americans. They contained misinformation specifically intended to corrupt our democratic process. Disinformation campaigns are rising with new actors, including the Chinese, attempting to influence US elections.

The Honest Ads Act modernizes campaign finance regulations and includes internet ads. Currently, mainstream media must follow the 2002 McCain-Feingold rules, but there is an internet loophole for online ads that were not a major political factor. If this legislation is implemented, internet ads would be required to tag on a disclaimer stating who paid for that ad.

The legislation was introduced by Senators Lindsey Graham (R-SC), Amy Klobuchar (D-MN), and Mark Warner (D-VA). The initiative enjoys bipartisan political support and is backed by Microsoft, Facebook, and Twitter but not Google or Amazon.

Trevor Potter, the Republican former chairperson of the Federal Election Committee, wrote this in support of the Honest Ads Act: "The 2016 elections exposed glaring holes in our ability to police foreign intervention in U.S. elections, and this bill is an appropriate, bipartisan disclosure remedy. Voters have a right to be fully informed about who is trying to influence their vote, particularly foreign powers whose motives are contrary to American interests. The Honest Ads Act gives voters, journalists, and law enforcement officers important tools to help root out all illegal foreign activity. The transparency this bill aims to provide in the 2018 elections and beyond will protect and enhance the integrity of our elections, which are the most fundamental component of American self-governance."[56]

A Final Note on Our Campaign Finance Differences

Perhaps you are thinking, and with good reason, that the differences between our solutions are too wide to bridge. Maybe you also feel the current campaign finance system is too broken to repair—that the incivility, lack of respect, and polarization that characterize our present political landscape are too deeply entrenched.

We do not believe that to be the case. We believe real change *is* possible, and the political environment is ripe for it. Throughout 2020 and 2021, we have lived through a recent series of shocks: the ugliness and polarization of the Trump Presidency, the Capitol Insurrection, both peaceful and violent social unrest on our streets, and the worldwide pandemic and resultant economic hardships. A destabilizing shock to a system can be a catalyst for fundamental change.

History is replete with examples of societies that have created systemic change after destabilizing shocks. Significant changes in how systems operate are usually the result of a jolt to equilibrium. This phenomenon occurs in business: iTunes fundamentally altered the music publishing industry and turned the business model on its head. Significant changes due to the status quo occur in nature and evolution. The peppered moths of Manchester are a case in point.

Before the industrial revolution in England, the moths of Manchester were predominantly pale and blended in well with the bark of the trees in the area. After the industrial revolution spewed pollution into the skies and trees, tree bark darkened. As a result, more pale-colored moths were eaten because they were no longer as effectively camouflaged. Darker, speckled moths that blended in with the soot-covered trees survived and passed on their genes. Within a few generations, the moths of Manchester were predominantly dark and peppered.

In that one example from nature, a dramatic shock to the environment caused a real and lasting change. Perhaps the recent shocks to the American psyche might cause a fundamental shift toward lasting respect through which we can reform the damaged parts of our collective minds and political system.

Chapter 9

COVID-19: A Perfect Example of Extreme Polarization

Duris our *Respect Retreat* at Ed's house in the summer of 2021, the three of us—Ed, Celinda, and Mo—spent our evenings sitting on a porch that looked out toward South Carolina's low country and debating the topics covered in this book. The discussions often went long into the night. We would gather again in Ed's kitchen for coffee and breakfast each morning. As soon as the caffeine hit our systems and our phones started beaming in emails and information from our respective offices, we resumed our debate. One morning, after once again staying up past midnight, clarifying our thoughts on how media silos perpetuated confirmation bias, a new discussion arose, centered on a topic that had occupied the national consciousness for over a year: COVID-19.

"I was thinking about your latest Battleground Poll," said Mo. "I found something telling. You started the focus groups by asking about polarization. They didn't immediately go into politics. They went to COVID."

"My office was conducting some new focus groups last night," Celinda said after consulting her phone. "Those participants did the same thing."

"What did they have to say?" asked Ed.

"They said their neighbors were shaming them for wearing masks," Celinda replied. "And plenty of people felt shamed for *not* wearing masks."

"People are at each other's throats about masks," Ed said.

"Mitch McConnell has just started using campaign funds to run ads in Kentucky encouraging people to get vaccinated," Mo chimed in.

"Really?" Celinda commented, somewhat surprised. "It'd be brilliant if more people were doing that instead of complaining about having to shut down again."

"It's not that they are complaining," Ed replied. "It's that they feel the government is punishing people that got vaccinated, are tired of masks, and want their businesses to open up again. They feel punished for doing the *right* thing, and that creates distrust."

"I'm sorry, I have a problem with 'this is just a government power grab' argument," Celinda said. "Masks and vaccine mandates could save lives. That's why we want them, not to infringe on people's rights."

"The bottom line is that if someone didn't get a vaccine, they sure aren't going to put a mask on because it's mandated again," Ed replied.

"We're all getting animated here, raising our voices as we're talking," Mo commented. "We've discussed so many different things this week, but somehow, this subject got us all fired up immediately. And your focus groups brought up COVID unprompted."

"It's inescapable," said Ed.

"More than that, I think it's the ultimate case study in our lack of respect," said Mo. "A crystal-clear distillation of the problems we've identified."

Indeed, the frustrations inherent in our discussion that morning in the summer of 2021 mirrored the attitude of many Americans. A new deadly strain of the virus, the Delta variant, had been wreaking havoc across the country, spreading new cases through states that had thought they were ready to reopen. Hospitals that believed they had seen the worst of the worst the previous winter were once again overrun with patients at death's door. Americans had been through sixteen months of isolation, economic hardship, and uncertainty. Now they had yet another challenge with which to contend. The emergence of the Delta variant felt like a re-visit of the same old miseries—a return to the endlessly repeating, confounding labyrinth that life under COVID-19 had become.

At the same time, our focus groups and polls showed that most people didn't focus their negative responses on the Delta variant, the pandemic's death toll, or its economic devastation. Perhaps those things were too much to process, or maybe people accepted them as the unavoidable fallout of a global pandemic. Instead, Americans grumbled about their neighbors' *mask-wearing practices* and lamented over *social media posts* by people they viewed as ignorant. They reserved their most fervent vitriol for the institutions they thought mishandled the situation. They blasted local and federal government mandates, or lack thereof, and out-of-touch officials and governors. They thought the media had missed the mark in its coverage, to put it charitably.

At an albeit prolonged moment in history, when Americans should have been uniting to fight a common though invisible enemy, we turned on our institutions and each other. That's not only dispiriting; it's a unique indictment of our contemporary polarization. We didn't always react to crises by digging deeper lines of division. When facing down the Axis of Evil in World War II, people planted victory gardens and women went to work in factories to replace the men who had been sent to battle. Just six weeks after Ronald Reagan was wounded in an assassination attempt, he pushed Congress to pass much-needed economic reform. After Jihadists flew passenger jets into the World Trade Center on 9/11, the country rallied behind New York City, and Americans came together with the unity that the times demanded. Sadly, we don't have to use much imagination to guess what would have happened if we hadn't united in those moments of history—because we are living through an example of that result.

Instead of banding together to fight a familiar foe, we have looked for culprits among our kind. The enemy is your neighbor who won't take the vaccine. Or the enemy is the health official who insists you must take the vaccine. It's the reckless governor of Florida. It's the business-shuttering governor of California. It's the parents who want their kids back in school. It's the schools that insist on staying closed for the safety of their teaching staff. It's the man who refuses to wear a mask in the supermarket. It's the clerk who yells at that man to put his [explicative] mask on. A person takes a video of this incident and posts it on Facebook. People write nasty comments under that Facebook video or even "like" the uncivil post. It can even be someone in your own family whose attitudes or actions you find objectionable.

The lines we've drawn against one another in response to COVID-19 ironically removed our last mask of civility, revealing extreme divisions that have been simmering for years. The polarization also serves as a perfect case study for the underlying issues we've spent the last eight chapters dissecting. It speaks to our broken problem-solving, upside-down structure, distrust of the media, and tendency to politicize every aspect of life. This chapter will examine how each of those factors has fractured our nation.

Politicizing a Disease

Most of us grew up with the rational and healthy belief that we should be vaccinated against diseases like polio for our good and the public good. That belief wasn't remotely controversial. Indeed, the idea that a medical emergency that affected the general population should have been bipartisan. Unfortunately, America never even reached that simple starting place of moving forward in ways that served the common good. Counter-intuitively, COVID-19 was politicized from the start.

Instead of holding a unified idea on how to approach this public health issue, Democrats and Republicans splintered among ideological lines. Many Democrats championed social distancing and mask-wearing with almost religious zeal. Many of those on the right side of the aisle framed the issue in terms of "government tyranny." To them, masks were muzzles to keep you in line rather than a tool that might help save lives. Sacrificing some aspects of behavior for our fellow Americans has morphed into a bizarre political game. Public servants who should have been working to protect their citizens and save their economic livelihoods focused on scoring political points with their base.

This divisiveness caused the public to retreat into political corners. In a September 2020 paper for *The Brooking Institute* titled "The Real Cost of Political Polarization: Evidence from the COVID-19 Pandemic,"[57] authors Jonathan Rothwell and Christos Makridis used data available from March to July 2020 on over

47,000 individuals to investigate how heterogeneity in beliefs about the pandemic corresponded to politics. What they found was that "partisan affiliation is often the strongest single predictor of behavior and attitudes about COVID-19, even more powerful than local infection rates or demographic characteristics, such as age and health status." The authors also showed how partisanship deeply impacted policy when they wrote, "A state's partisan orientation also explains its public health policies, including the timing and duration of stay-at-home orders, bans on the social gathering, and mask mandates."

Rothwell and Makridis found that both sides continued this political gamesmanship long into the pandemic. In a September 2020 study, undertaken more than six months after the crisis began, they documented, "In Democratic areas, there is still considerable pressure to keep organizations and businesses closed, especially schools, and we've even seen recent calls to shut down the entire economy once again. These ideas strike us as unfortunate reactions based on distrust of the president rather than proposals grounded in evidence. As one of us has noted through Gallup's partnership with Franklin-Templeton to study COVID, Democrats are more likely than Republicans to overstate the risks of death to young people. . . . In contrast, Republicans are more likely to believe that the flu is more deadly than COVID mistakenly."

Why did our leaders play politics instead of helping a public that was quite literally dying? They did so because they were rewarded for it. The broken incentive structure we examined in Chapter Four didn't disappear just because of this dangerous virus. Instead of producing a sound policy, this divisive rhetoric and grandstanding garnered more support. Many leaders leaned into the worst angels of their nature and benefited from doing so.

In a September 2021 paper titled "Why Has COVID and the Response to COVID Become so Political?" Brent Nelsen, professor of Politics and International Affairs at Furman University, wrote, "Vaccines and masks are not seen as apolitical solutions to an apolitical, technical problem that needs to be solved by experts and technocrats. No, scientific evidence is now seen through partisan lenses, allowing both sides to claim scientific backing for their political preferences. Today's political incentives push politicians to make every national issue a wedge that further pushes American citizens to one camp or another. These incentives are boosted by powerful cultural forces that act like political steroids."[58]

As the pandemic-saturated months stretched on and more Americans died, our national polarization grew ever more extreme and filtered into one of the few aspects of American life untouched by politics—our health. "Partisanship is now the strongest and most consistent divider in health behaviors," Shana Gadarian, a political scientist at Syracuse University, told Vox for a July 2021 story titled "How Political Polarization Broke America's Vaccine Campaign."[59] It may be as disturbing to you as it is to us that people would risk their *lives* based on their ideology, but that reality became increasingly commonplace. People's scientific beliefs also bled into their politics; that same Vox piece reported that people's vaccinated status is a better predictor of states' electoral outcomes than their votes in prior elections.

Sadly, as of this writing, the politicization of COVID-19 is still as strong as ever. If you turn on C-SPAN, you'll see that every Democratic senator on the floor wears a mask, and every Republican's face is bare. It's a clear example of how ideologically-centered politics have come to define this disease and this national tragedy.

Ed Asks If Trump was the Symptom or the Disease

By this point, you may be wondering why we haven't addressed the elephant in the room regarding COVID-19: Donald Trump. In this book, we've purposefully kept our discussion of Trump limited, in the belief that his follies are well documented and best left in the rear-view mirror if the country is to move forward and build upon a foundation of respect. But the fact of the matter is that President Trump held this nation's highest office for much of the pandemic and mishandled it in many ways, especially when it came to vaccine efforts. We both believe we still have so many people unvaccinated because of Donald Trump.

Yet Trump's handling of the pandemic was not unexpected. He acted like Donald Trump. There is a more profound question to be asked here, a question Ed asked the students who took part in an eight-week discussion group on civility he led as part of his fellowship at the Georgetown Institute of Politics and Public Service. *Is Donald Trump a symptom of the disease or the disease itself?*

My students viewed Trump as one *symptom* of a more extensive disease that has infected our culture, although a significant one. The prevailing sentiment among them was that Trump reflects broader issues and divides within our society while offering them an emboldened permissiveness. One student said, "I would call him a symptom, but more like a high fever than a runny nose. You can give it medicine for a runny nose, and it will be fine in a couple of days; you don't have to do anything. But with a high fever, you have to go to the hospital."

Of course, I agree with my students. They had grown up in a polarized nation and were wise beyond their years. They knew that seeds of the division had been planted for a long time. Trump just watered them with a firehouse.

My students at Georgetown inspired me to ask voters in our Battleground Poll a version of this same question: *Is Trump the symptom or the disease?* Voters were split on whether he was one of the causes of the rise in divisiveness or if he was a byproduct of a country that was already fracturing. At the same time, almost all voters we polled agreed that some of former President Trump's actions contributed to the problem of incivility and division.

When we asked a group of Biden voters, the feeling was unanimous. Independents were split on whether Trump was the cause of the acceleration of incivility in the country or he was just a byproduct of a more significant trend. Trump voters were more likely to say the country was headed in this direction even before Trump, while Biden voters were more likely to say that Trump was a major cause of division. Some Biden voters pointed to the January 6 insurrection as an example of Trump directly causing division that would likely not have otherwise happened. Below are some telling responses:

I think Trump had a hand in it [the rise of incivility].
(Independent Senior)

It [Trump] escalated it. I think we were already headed in that direction. We were going that way before all of this, but that certainly did not help anything.
(Independent Senior)

Many participants traced the incivility and division in the government to the disrespect and division in their own homes. Some independents had a rule in their family not to talk about politics to keep the peace and avoid fighting. Other voters spoke about how their politics impacted their work and caused them to lose revenue when clients discovered their politics. However, some voters didn't see the civility problem as personal but a problem that existed across the country and government. Donald Trump was a grand reveal. He exposed divisions that already existed and used them for political purposes. He legitimized, expanded, and weaponized those divisions between people, individuals, and groups.

Politics has become entertainment, and Trump played to that. Today, the consumer hungers for sensationalism over substance in the media and confrontation over civility. Trump used his version of identity politics to drive a wedge between groups, fostering an "us against them" mentality. This fueled moral righteousness in politics, with people refusing to engage in civil discussions because of their "strong moral belief" in their political perspective. In essence, the thought is, if you attack my ideas, you attack me—and you attack America. Trump both mirrored and advanced our current political polarization and allegiance.

Over half of Americans believe political violence will increase, while less than 20 percent think it will decrease. Now the enemies of democracy lie within. Seven in ten people we polled believe democracy is threatened. Perhaps most shocking of all, 54 percent of Americans think *other Americans* are the biggest threat to our country. We have met the enemy, and they are ours.[60]

I believed long ago that Trump was the symptom but not the disease. My resolve to address civility and respect was driven by the fear that for so many of our voters to accept the style and persona of Donald Trump meant our nation had devolved to a level of acceptance in incivility that is genuinely alarming. Given that this spiritual disease had been simmering under the surface for years, it's no surprise to me that an *actual* disease divided the country even further. I wish it hadn't happened that way, but maybe this is necessary to realize that we need to inoculate ourselves against hyper-polarization. As the pandemic has shown us, our very lives depend on it.

Celinda Looks at an Example Set by Women

I want to inject a ray of hope into this sobering and much-needed examination of the pandemic. Women play a crucial role here, which might inspire us to move forward.

Part of the beginning of the demise of Donald Trump was due to many women voters who had become disenchanted with his style. At first, they thought Trump wasn't a politician, and for that reason, spoke for them directly. His leadership took an ominous turn when he used division to govern for political gain. Initially, these women had trouble with his style but still stuck with him because they agreed with his agenda. Then COVID-19 hit, and these women watched his petty and egotistical governing style every night on TV. His unnecessary and inappropriate dressing-down of nurses, CDC officials, and others trying to get the pandemic under control hindered our response to the virus's rapid spread, impeding policy implementation and ultimately damaging the country.

Females didn't like his style because women always want to bring people together. We see ourselves as the uniters, the peace-makers, in everything from Thanksgiving dinner to politics. Women understand that we can't get things done unless we work together—at the family level, the community level, and the national governing level.

Polling Data Shows Battle Fatigue

Haven't we had enough of the polarization and incivility that threatens the integrity of our presidential elections? Polling data from our latest Battleground suggests Americans are tired of the fighting, finger-pointing, and dysfunction in Washington, DC. Our polls showed that some voters were optimistic, feeling like the worst of the pandemic was behind the country and America was beginning to heal. Biden's win and the change in administration helped support those upbeat feelings. Our focus groups also showed us that people want strong, decisive, decent leaders who are open to compromise and filled with empathy. Here are some of their responses:

I think open and honest, as long as you have that open honesty. I do think that thinking before you speak is really important. I'd like to see that with our leaders, having well thought out, articulate, not just saying the first thing that comes to mind. (Independent Woman)

I want someone who's compassionate. I want a leader that shares my same values or at least is open-minded. Things change so much, so I want someone that's informed, not just with us as a country, but as a nation, because we all have to work together. (Independent Woman)

Any signs of optimism in these troubled times are encouraging. Neither of us wants our country to revert to an earlier era of homogeneity and restrictive racial and social hierarchies. Instead, we want to and, for the sake of our democracy, *must* look forward to a time of diversity and equality. We are a nation of immigrants, a country of contradictions and competing interests, a nation of stunning ingenuity and innovation, and a nation of vile racism and stupidity. With all these sometimes disparate characteristics, still, we as a nation have worked together to create a land of freedom and opportunity—something too precious to destroy for the sake of those with a selfish and short-sighted agenda.

A Final Word of Warning

We realize any discussion about the pandemic can seem much like the pandemic itself: a never-ending stream of negative information without much in the way of solutions. To be candid, during our Respect Retreat in South Carolina, we realized that any answers we agreed upon seem insignificant against the magnitude of the myriad of problems COVID-19 has brought to the surface. What we have tried to do throughout this book is take a hard and honest look at those problems and challenges. We hope that by turning the mirror on ourselves, we might all wake up to the *severity* of the situation. If this chapter seemed grim, it's because we intended it to be. We hope it's a reality check that shows how bad things have become.

Now let's end with some signs that all is far from lost—that respect will prevail, thanks to some glowing lights at the end of this dark tunnel we are all in at this very moment.

Chapter 10

Looking Toward
a Respectful Future

Our hope with this book is that the issues raised in the previous chapters have inspired your concern and reflection. Critical analysis always precedes change. At the same time, we recognize that a widespread reorganization of our national values around respect will require action from institutions and individuals. Admitting American malice and mutual disrespect is, in some ways, easy enough. Amending it, however, will take sustained effort. Unfortunately, we have not had a groundswell of support from our current elected leaders in this direction. Consumed by partisan bickering, protected in their media silos, many are now accustomed to offensive and defensive incivility. Who then will take up this mantle?

The most obvious answer, for us, is the American youth. We come from an activist youth ourselves. We were in high school in the sixties, graduating at the height of the anti-war movement— another troubled time in our nation's history. Our college years began with the tragedy of Kent State, which brought more voices both onto the streets and college campuses but also found many students looking for ways to have their voices heard through more traditional routes.

Today's youth are no less passionate than those who walked before them. Many look back at the anti-war movement as representative of their ideals—human rights and respect for our fellow Americans. The actions of young people will be critical to cementing respect as a core value of our democracy. We believe the endeavor's success depends heavily on their focus and commitment. We as a nation will also need elected leaders to stand up for civility and respect rather than continue to fight in the trenches of partisan divides—leaders that will light the way for our youth. Still, we feel they have an excellent opportunity to spur a movement in universities and that this will spill out into workplaces and communities.

The American people seem to agree. In our January 2022 Battleground poll, 58 percent of the public said, "Young people are the best hope for the future." Young people themselves overwhelmingly answered this question in the affirmative. That's critical. It means the youth are confident they are the ones for the job. Instead of spinning into nihilism, they've remained optimistic about their ability. Hearteningly, they have support from seniors.

Fascinated by the response to that Battleground Poll, we engaged directly with young people. In March 2022, we set up a focus group at Georgetown University with ten college-age Georgetown students and conducted seven one-on-one interviews with younger non-college adults. Those individual interviews were with non-students from California, South Dakota, Florida, North Carolina, Ohio, and Pennsylvania. The students in the Georgetown focus group were from various political parties and originally from

New York, West Virginia, Georgia, Missouri, Ohio, DC, Arizona, and Florida. The one-on-one non-student interviews and the focus group of college students were both of mixed gender and race. All interviewees had at least a high school degree, but none had a bachelor's or four-year college degree.

We told each participant or group about our relationship to open the interviews—how it had always been based on mutual respect. "Ed and I have worked together for decades, more decades than you are old, so that's how long it's been," Celinda said. "We met in a bar in Budapest when the US was helping to build democracy in Hungary." We told them we were writing a book about respect and had them read the first chapter before the interviews. In the focus groups, we made it clear that we weren't interested in academic responses; we weren't there to delve into the study presented in their sociology course or debate the latest *New York Times* article. And we weren't looking for consensus. We wanted their gut impressions. We told them we encouraged respectful disagreement.

It's fair to say these young people rose to that challenge far better than most of our leadership, albeit in a controlled setting. The conversations proved illuminating and encouraging. Since the number of participants was limited, we won't present the work as quantitative. However, we *can* feel confident saying these young people had an excellent handle on much of what is in this book.

One of the first things we had them respond to was the Battleground data that inspired the majority consensus in our 2002 Battleground Poll. "Fifty-eight percent of the public feels that young people are the best hope for the country's future," we told them. "How does that make you feel? What do you think?"

"I think it makes me angry," a woman named Amimi responded. "Not to put the blame on older generations, but it almost feels like they're shifting the burden of the responsibilities to make a change on us. But it also gives me a sense of urgency because I think pretty much every young person that I know wants to make a change."

Amimi's call for change was ubiquitous among the participants. They expressed that sentiment more frequently and ardently than any other age group. Yet, almost unanimously, they also felt this would be difficult, and the country wasn't headed in the right direction. Amimi's anger was not uncommon. Across the board, the Georgetown student group and the feelings about the country's direction exhibited a mix of nervousness and anxiety, frustration and disappointment.

"I would say I feel stuck. Yeah, it's just like a stalemate," said Louis, a young student from Colorado.

"I would say I feel irritated because I feel like there are some decisions that we could make that are more moral choices," said a non-college student named Michael.

The negative feelings exhibited generally centered around their sense that the government was not getting anything done. They shared a familiar feeling that division had worsened in the country and politics were too polarizing. "I think humanity has been taken up by politics; humanity has been taken out," reflected a young male student named J.K.

In particular, participants in the Georgetown group worried the US was losing what little middle ground we had left, and it was becoming a battle between two sides who were finding it impossible under the present conditions to understand each other. "This is something that I saw firsthand in my country, Venezuela. I was born and raised there," shared a young woman named Maria Victoria. "I still have family there who experienced intolerance from the Chavistas, the left socialist wing in the country, and from the opposition party.

There's no middle there, like the middle completely does not exist in Venezuela. That is something that I've seen that has been happening in this country. The divide has been getting more polarized, so that's something that worries me because once you stop having a middle, once you stop in the game for so long that they've used up their good ideas. So it's time for someone else," she said.

"Well, I think we haven't seen much change because our government's so old. Like they don't really understand how to use social media," commented a liberal arts student named Nicolette.

We were curious to see what changes these young adults hoped for from the new leadership. Changing the guard is one thing. What happens next is something else entirely. All of the participants believed in human rights as fundamental to a democracy. They felt all people, as human beings, deserve equality. "I'm personally energized by a lot of people in our generation in terms of understanding that civil rights and human rights don't have to be a political issue," said Nicolette. They saw respect as a core value, bringing a smile to our faces. Respect was a common idea that these participants thought could unite people across party lines.

Nonetheless, all involved were more divided on how that respect was obtained. "I would say that the first principle of respect is to recognize the humanity in everybody, and that can be very difficult," Amimi admitted. All agreed that it is essential to have empathy, listen, and be open-minded to foster that respect.

Half of the participants believed respect should automatically be given to everyone as a fellow human being in the Georgetown group. Others in the group felt that respect must be *earned*. "Those who would deny me *my* identity do not deserve my respect," was a common refrain. It's hard to maintain a mutual level of respect when you see me as less than a human," said Ada.

This topic of defining respect was of great interest to us. We saw the students as challenging us to understand what genuine respect means and, at the same time, having hope for a future where we can get this dynamic under control. The core danger we envision for this generation is this breakdown—the lack of respect. As it is, many people feel they can act with disrespect because they believe someone else or some others have violated their basic humanity.

In dealing with this question and advising young people, we begin with a more straightforward definition of respect. We believe we need to respect each other *until* we give each other a reason not to. The word "until" is the critical part of the definition. It means that we benefit from open-minded listening with our fellow Americans whenever we engage in discourse—on the world stage and in our living rooms and dining tables. We believe in this definition of respect at our very core. We were raised that way, and that's how we conduct ourselves. Today, most Democrats don't expect open-mindedness and core respect from Republicans, nor do Republicans expect that from Democrats or those more progressive. Yet this expectation of what's needed—and what's still possible—is one of the anchors of our friendship and what has brought us to write this book. If there is one thesis here, one takeaway that we want to impart to young people, it's this: *Start from respect.*

As the conversations at Georgetown continued, they became brainstorming sessions to help us find possible solutions to the issues we presented in the book. Social media was a rich vein of discussion. Social networks are young people's first language, and because they use them constantly, they understand how they play such a massive role in the division.

"I am going to get you guys to fix social media," Ed jokingly advised. They were pretty serious about taking on this responsibility since their fluency made them astute about the possible solutions for the great divide in social media. They wanted to hold both those online platforms *and* each other accountable. They said social media companies need to do better at content moderation, blocking misinformation and content that reinforces hateful ideas. That's not surprising, as most young people hold those views and are less concerned than other demographics that hold up their concept of what they see as the need for "absolute free speech on social media." Perhaps it is surprising that some of these young people volunteered to change *their* behavior. They talked about different personal experiments, such as taking breaks from social media and sharing and forwarding fewer possible divisive things. Several even took it beyond the idea of individual experiments and posed the idea of starting a broader action addressing algorithm reform, which we found intriguing.

Some in the Georgetown group saw these discussions as an example of how talking through the issues and listening to others' points of view was a strategy that could help bridge the vast polarization gap. As a young man named Brady said, "I am just so impressed with all the students, with all of us here in this conversation, and just how thoughtful everybody has been. That really gives me hope for the country."

Listening to problems and solutions from their peers made these participants hopeful for their generation, as everyone's concerns seemed legitimate, even if those issues hadn't been of previous concern to others. No one saw their generation as superheroes that could instantly go out and make the world better. They did view their generation as composed of individuals who could listen, learn, and have a diverse variety of solutions. "I don't think we're some saviors who have been gifted. I truly believe most Americans inherently feel that way," Brady continued.

J.K. also powerfully voiced that same optimistic sentiment and willingness to be open-minded and inclusive. "I honor you all," he said to his fellow students. "I honor your resistance. I honor your story. I honor your background. And in that, if I were ever put in a position where we needed to create public policy, create regulation, and make a judgment, I honor you guys to the degree where I can compromise my own experience with an understanding that we come to a place, not within the farthest mindset, but to make things better for everyone else."

These participants felt it was possible to find common ground even while disagreeing on significant issues. They held that their generation was the one to fix many aspects of a broken political system through respect, shared understanding, and listening. "I would say [respect] is something you have to choose every day," said Maria Victoria. "It's not something you can just put in the back of your mind, but something you have to choose."

We held these focus groups to see how big a wall has been built between the generations. Our conclusion, in the end, was that there isn't as much of a wall as we thought. These young people, and their peers, are profoundly committed to the future of America. It is encouraging that 58 percent of the public believes they are our best hope for the future. You can put us firmly in that camp.

The Role of Leadership

Of course, young people cannot rise to the moment's challenge alone. They will need not only allies but *leaders,* who will step up and light the way with a firm commitment to respectful civil discourse in the public arena. One comment from J.K., the only young optimist, struck a chord with us. "Now, what we do have to recognize and realize, though, is that we must elect, and we must empower, good, ethical, and smart people to help us through these moments," he said. "And that's why I am so optimistic."

J.K. is wise beyond his years. A youth movement toward civility and respect needs experienced leaders committed to those specific goals. What would leaders like that look like? Indeed, there seems to be a shortage of such people today. As we are no longer young ourselves, we look to inspiration from the great uniters of our generation—people like John McCain.

John McCain was a public servant who served the country in war and peace. He saw man's inhumanity at its worst as a POW in Vietnam. This experience drove him to always strive to treat his fellow men and women with dignity and respect. He was a champion of civility. During the dog days of the 2008 presidential race, a voter at a Minnesota rally accused Barack Obama of being someone who "cohorts with domestic terrorists."

It was three weeks before voters would decide the presidency, and McCain was trailing in the polls. This was an opportunity to encourage the worst impulses of some of his followers and perhaps gain some much-needed political firepower in the process. Instead, he came to his opponent's defense. "I have to tell you," he replied, "he is a decent person, and a person you do not have to be scared of as [the] president of the United States."

The crowd immediately booed. McCain paused and raised his hand toward his temples, clearly upset with the incivility of the moment. But he continued extolling the value of disagreeing with Obama's ideas while respecting him as an American. Later in the rally, he brought the woman on stage who called Obama an "Arab."

Shaking his head vigorously, McCain gently took the microphone back from her. "No, ma'am," he said.

"No?" she pressed.

"No, ma'am," he insisted. "He's a decent family man [and] citizen I just happen to have disagreements with on fundamental issues."[61]

Until his final breath, McCain continued living by this code of respect. In his farewell statement that he wrote for the public, he reaffirmed those values. "'Fellow Americans'—that association has meant more to me than any other," he wrote. "We are three-hundred-and-twenty-five million opinionated, vociferous individuals. We argue, compete, and sometimes even vilify each other in our raucous public debates. But we have always had so much more in common than in disagreement. Do not despair of our present difficulties, but always believe in the promise and greatness of America because nothing is inevitable here. Americans never quit. We never surrender. We never hide from history. We make history."[62]

So how do we "make history" to echo McCain's eternal words? We need new leaders to surface and continue McCain's legacy. They need to be leaders who not only appeal to young people but also people's better angels and light the path to a more civil, more respectful nation. We agreed with our focus group when they said that college-age people like themselves aren't going to be motivated by yet another older adult in a suit. Perhaps this seems unfair, but it's honest. One politician who might be a fruitful example is Pete Buttigieg. We already discussed Mayor Pete's campaign Rules of the Road. His continued application of those values since his presidential run is heartening.

We realize these leaders will not simply surface out of the blue. They must be found, fostered, and given every opportunity to speak to and appeal to young people. Perhaps as pollsters, this is one place where we can be of some small service to our country here. While we have no interest in being political leaders ourselves, we can facilitate that leadership. One of the jobs we have as pollsters is to have our radar on to catch new movements to be incorporated into each party's structure and strategy. Scores of people—certainly not just the young people—are feeling the need for all of us to put more focus on less division and more focus on respect. Happily, we can report that this imperative is organically growing in colleges across America. There are a growing number of programs at universities around the country focusing on civility and polarization—from our colleague Mo Elleithee's program at Georgetown to the University of Delaware's Biden School Ithaca Initiative, to the National Institute for Civil Discourse at the University of Arizona. These programs are all coming at a critical time, not only engaging with the students on each campus but also with each other, laying the foundation for a national movement born in our universities and driven by students who want to see things change. As pollsters, we can take the pulse of the electorate. In so doing, we are informing the candidates we work with that people truly hunger for a more civil discourse focused on solutions, not division and ugliness, and we see that playing a more significant role in their final vote decision.

Our Final Note

The process of writing this book has changed our relationship. Through this two-year writing process, we've come to understand each other even better. Before starting this journey, we didn't fully grasp how much our shared views on respect were reinforced by our parents and the core values they instilled in us. That was interesting because one family, Celinda's, was Republican while Ed's family was Democrat, and we each switched parties. Having that earlier affiliation and growing an inside perspective was of great benefit.

What we loved about each other from the beginning was that, at our roots, we committed to what we believed in. We treated each other respectfully because we saw those as humanistic concerns and commitments rather than simply our positions on various political and social issues.

When we decided to write a book that dealt with sensitive and often contentious political issues, our positions were not always aligned. We had to figure out how to compromise and keep the focus not on our political disagreements but on our mutual objective of championing respect. We learned that strong leadership means leaving room for others to offer differing opinions in an atmosphere of mutual respect and willingness to keep an open mind—and, where necessary, find fertile common ground that provides the best for most people.

We still have areas of disagreement. We always will. But we will always hear each other out. We will not be angry, insulting, or dismissive. We will bring our respect for each other to every interaction, every poll we do together, every piece of campaign advice we give our clients, and every mentorship we undertake. Fundamental to our relations is this commitment we share: we are both concerned citizens who want nothing more than to make life better for others. Hopefully, after reading this book, you will feel the same about those in your life and on your ballots.

Thank you, dear reader, for listening so respectfully.

About the Authors

ED GOEAS

E d Goeas is president and CEO of The Tarrance Group, one of the most respected and successful Republican survey research and strategy teams in American politics. They serve as the pollster for thirty current members of the US House of Representatives, twelve US senators, and five governors. Over the last thirty years, the team at The Tarrance Group has elected hundreds of members of the US House of Representatives, dozens of US senators, numerous governors, along with countless statewide officeholders.

In recognition of the number of winning campaigns conducted by The Tarrance Group, Ed and his partners, Brian Tringali and Dave Sackett, were honored as "2010 Republican Pollster of the Year" and "2014 Republican Pollster of the Year" by the American Association of Political Consultants (AAPC).

Ed is also widely recognized as one of the country's leading political strategists.

Ed has done extensive survey research on health care, criminal justice reform, immigration reform, education, young voters or youth, and populism over the years. He was program director for the 2008 Republican National Convention for John McCain. On the Board of Directors for the American Association of Political Consultants for twenty-five years, he was the longest-serving member of the Board, focusing his efforts on campaign ethics and promoting increased youth participation in the industry.

In addition to his campaign work, Goeas works in partnership with Democratic pollster Celinda Lake on the nationally recognized "Georgetown University Institute of Politics and Public Service Battleground Poll," one of the country's most respected national political research programs. In 2011, Lake and Goeas were awarded the "Distinguished Service to the Profession Award" for their body of work on the Battleground Poll over the last twenty years.

CELINDA LAKE

Celinda Lake is one of the Democratic Party's leading political strategists, having served as one of the top two pollsters for the Biden campaign, and continues to work for the DNC. She works for the national party committees and dozens of Democratic incumbents and challengers. Celinda and her firm, Lake Research Partners, are known for cutting-edge research on issues, including the economy, health care, the environment, and education, and have worked for several institutions, including the Democratic Attorneys General Association, AFL-CIO, SEIU, NRDC, ecoAmerica, NARAL, Planned

Parenthood, EMILY's List, and the Barbara Lee Family Foundation. Her international work has included work in Liberia, Belarus, Ukraine, South Africa, and Central America. During the 1992 election cycle, Celinda oversaw focus group research for the Clinton-Gore campaign. In 2005, she and Kellyanne Conway published *What Women Really Want*, which examines the ways women are changing the political landscape in America. Celinda is one of the nation's foremost experts on framing issues for women voters and has elected more women to office than any other firm in the country.

Celinda, a native of Montana—born and raised on a ranch—and one of the political world's most avid whitewater rafters, holds a Master's Degree in Political Science and Survey Research from the University of Michigan at Ann Arbor and a certificate in Political Science from the University of Geneva in Switzerland. Celinda received her undergraduate degree from Smith College in Massachusetts and was recently awarded the Distinguished Alumna Medal. She received the lifetime achievement award from the American Association of Political Consultants (AAPC) with Republican Ed Goeas for her work on the Battleground Poll. A resident of Washington, DC, Celinda enjoys fishing, traveling, cooking, attending craft shows and dance concerts, and spending time with friends in her free time.

MO ELLEITHEE

Mo Elleithee is an American political campaign strategist. A Democrat, he has served as spokesman for the Democratic National Committee, Hillary Clinton, and other Democratic elected officials and organizations. He is currently executive director of the Institute of

Politics and Public Service at Georgetown University. In 2016, he became a FOX News political contributor.

Mo Elleithee is the founding executive director of Georgetown University's Institute of Politics and Public Service, the first institute of its kind in the nation's capital.

Before launching the institute in 2015, Mo spent two decades as one of the top communications strategists in the Democratic Party, most recently as communications director and chief spokesman of the Democratic National Committee.

A veteran of four presidential campaigns, Mo was senior spokesman and traveling press secretary on Hillary Clinton's 2008 campaign. He served as a senior advisor and strategist for Senator Tim Kaine's campaigns for governor and US Senate and has worked on numerous other statewide and local races in every region of the country.

A frequent political commentator on television and radio, Mo was named a FOX News contributor in 2016. He was a founding partner of Hilltop Public Solutions, one of Washington's leading political consulting and public affairs firms. He's been recognized on *Washington Life* magazine's "Power 100" list; as a "Top Influencer" by *Campaigns & Elections* magazine and featured on *Washingtonian* magazine's "Guest List."

Appendix #1

Joe Biden's Eulogy for John McCain

"**M**y name is Joe Biden. I'm a Democrat. And I loved John McCain. I have had the dubious honor over the years of giving some eulogies for fine women and men that I've admired. But, Lindsey, this one's hard.

"The three men who spoke before me, I think, captured John, different aspects of John in a way that only someone close to him could understand. But the way I look at it, the way I thought about it, was that I always thought of John as a brother. We had a [heck] of a lot of family fights. We go back a long way. I was a young United States Senator. I got elected when I was twenty-nine. I had the dubious distinction of being put on the formulations committee, which the next youngest person was fourteen years older than me. And I spent a lot of time traveling the world because I was assigned responsibility, my colleagues in the Senate knew I was chairman of the European Affairs subcommittee, so I spent a lot of time at NATO and then the Soviet Union.

"Along came a guy a couple of years later, a guy I knew of, admired from afar, your husband, who had been a prisoner of war, who had endured enormous, enormous pain and suffering. And demonstrated the code, the McCain code. People don't think much about it today, but imagine having already known the pain you were likely to endure, and being offered the opportunity to go home, but saying no. As his son can tell you in the Navy, last one in, last one out.

"So I knew of John, and John became the Navy liaison officer in the United States Senate. There's an office, then it used to be on the basement floor, of members of the military who are assigned to senators when they travel abroad to meet with heads of state or other foreign dignitaries. And John had been recently released from the Hanoi Hilton, a genuine hero, and he became the Navy liaison. For some reason, we hit it off in the beginning. We were both full of dreams and ambitions and an overwhelming desire to make the time we had there worthwhile. To try to do the right thing. To think about how we could make things better for the country we loved so much.

"John and I ended up traveling every time I went anywhere. I took John with me or John took me with him. We were in China, Japan, Russia, Germany, France, England, Turkey, all over the world. Tens of thousands of miles. And we would sit on that plane and late into the night, when everyone else was asleep, and just talk. Getting to know one another. We'd talk about family, we'd talk about politics, we'd talk about international relations. We'd talk about promise, the promise of America. Because we were both cockeyed optimists and believe there's not a single thing beyond the capacity of this country. I mean, for real, not a single thing.

"And when you get to know another woman or man, you begin to know their hopes and their fears; you get to know their family even before you meet them; you get to know how they feel about important things. We talked about everything except captivity and the loss of my family which had just occurred, my wife and daughter, the only two things we didn't talk about.

"But I found that it wasn't too long into John's duties that Jill and I got married. Jill is here with me today. Five years, I had been a single dad, and no man deserves one great love, let alone two. And I met Jill. It changed my life. She fell in love with him and he with her. He'd always call her, as Lindsey would travel with her, Jilly. Matter of fact, when they got bored being with me on these trips, I remember in Greece, he said, 'Why don't I take Jill for dinner?' Later, I would learn they are at a cafe at the port and he has her dancing on top of a cement table drinking ouzo. Not a joke. Jilly. Right, Jilly?

"But we got to know each other well, and he loved my son Beau and my son Hunt. As a young man, he came up to my house, and he came up to Wilmington and out of this grew a great friendship that transcended whatever political differences we had or later developed because, above all, above all, we understood the same thing. All politics is personal. It's all about trust. I trusted John with my life and I would, and I think he would trust me with his. And as our life progressed, we learned more, there are times when life can be so cruel, pain so blinding, it's hard to see anything else.

"The disease that took John's life took our mutual friend's, Teddy [Kennedy]'s life, the exact same disease nine years ago, a couple days ago, and three years ago, took my beautiful son Beau's life. It's brutal. It's relentless. It's unforgiving. And it takes so much from those we love and from the families who love them that in order to survive, we have to remember how they lived, not how they died. I carry with me an image of Beau, sitting out in a little lake we live on, starting a motor on an old boat and smiling away. Not the last days. I'm sure Vickie Kennedy has her own image, looking, seeing Teddy looking so alive in a sailboat, out in the Cape. For the family, you will all find your own images, whether it's remembering his smile, his laugh or that touch in the shoulder or running his hand down your cheek. Or, just feeling like someone is looking, turn and see him just smiling at you, from a distance, just looking at you. Or when you saw the pure joy the moment he was about to take the stage on the Senate floor and start a fight.

"[Gosh], he loved it. So to Cindy, the kids, Doug, Andy, Cindy, Meghan, Jack, Jimmy, Bridget, and I know she's not here, but to Mrs. McCain, we know how difficult it is to bury a child, Mrs. McCain. My heart goes out to you. And I know right now, the pain you all are feeling is so sharp and so hollowing. And John's absence is all-consuming, for all of you right now. It's like being sucked into a black hole inside your chest. And it's frightening. But I know something else, unfortunately, from experience. There's nothing anyone can say or do to ease the pain right now. But I pray, I pray you take some comfort knowing that because you shared John with all of us, your whole life, the world now shares with you in the ache of John's death.

"Look around this magnificent church. Look what you saw coming from the state Capitol yesterday. It's hard to stand there but part of it, part of it was at least it was for me with Beau, standing in the state Capitol, you knew. It was genuine. It was deep. He touched so many lives. I've gotten calls not just because people knew we were friends, not just from people around the country, but leaders around the world calling. Meghan, I'm getting all these sympathy letters. I mean, hundreds of them, and tweets.

"Character is destiny. John had character. While others will miss his leadership, passion, even his stubbornness, you are going to miss that hand on your shoulder. Family, you are going to miss the man, faithful man as he was, who you knew would literally give his life for you. And for that, there's no balm but time. Time and your memories of a life lived well and lived fully.

"But I make you a promise. I promise you; the time will come that what's going to happen is six months will go by and everybody is going to think, well, it's passed. But you are going to ride by that field or smell that fragrance or see that flashing image. You are going to feel like you did the day you got the news. But you know you are going to make it. The image of your dad, your husband, your friend. It crosses your mind, and a smile comes to your lips before a tear to your eye. That's who you know. I promise you, I give you my word, I promise you, this I know. The day will come. That day will come.

"You know, I'm sure if my former colleagues who worked with John, I'm sure there's people who said to you not only now, but the last ten years, 'Explain this guy to me.' Right? Explain this guy to me. Because, as they looked at him, in one sense they admired him, in one sense, the way things changed so much in America, they look add him as if John came from another age, lived by a different code, an ancient, antiquated courage, integrity, duty, were alive. That was obvious how John lived his life. The truth is, John's code was ageless, is ageless. When you talked earlier, Grant, you talked about values. It wasn't about politics with John. He could disagree on substance, but the underlying values that animated everything John did, everything he was, come to a different conclusion. He'd part company with you, if you lacked the basic values of decency, respect, knowing this project is bigger than yourself.

"John's story is an American story. It's not hyperbole. It's the American story, grounded in respect and decency, basic fairness, the intolerance through the abuse of power. Many of you travel the world—look how the rest of the world looks at us. They look at us as little naïve, so fair, so decent. We are the naïve Americans. That's who we are. That's who John was. He could not stand the abuse of power—wherever he saw it, in whatever form, in whatever ways. He loved basic values, fairness, honesty, dignity, respect, giving hate no safe harbor, leaving no one behind and understanding Americans were part of something much bigger than ourselves.

"With John, it was a value set that was neither selfish nor self-serving. John understood that America was, first and foremost, an idea. Audacious and risky, organized around not tribe but ideals. Think of how he approached every issue. The ideals that Americans rallied around for 200 years, the ideals of the world have prepared you. Sounds corny. We hold these truths self-evident, that all men are created equal, endowed by their creator with certain rights. To John, those words had meaning, as they have for every great patriot who's ever served this country. We both loved the Senate. The proudest years of my life were being a United States Senator. I was honored to be Vice President, but a United States Senator. We both lamented, watching it change. During the long debates in the '80s and '90s, I would go sit next to John, next to his seat or he would come on the Democratic side and sit next to me. I'm not joking. We'd sit there and talk to each other. I came out to see John, we were reminiscing around it. It was '96, about to go to the caucus. We both went into our caucus and coincidentally, we were approached by our caucus leaders with the same thing. Joe, it doesn't look good, you sitting next to John all the time. I swear to G**, same thing was said to John in your caucus.

"That's when things began to change for the worse in America in the Senate. That's when it changed. What happened was, at those times, it was always appropriate to challenge another Senator's judgment, but never appropriate to challenge their motive. When you challenge their motive, it's impossible to get to go. If I say you are going this because you are being paid off or you are doing it because you are not a good Christian or this, that, or the other thing, it's impossible to reach consensus. Think about in your personal lives. All we do today is attack the oppositions of both parties, their motives, not the substance of their argument. This is the mid-'90s. It began to go downhill from there. The last day John was on the Senate floor, what was he fighting to do? He was fighting to restore what you call regular order, just start to treat one another again, like we used to.

"The Senate was never perfect, John, you know that. We were there a long time together. I watched Teddy Kennedy and James O. Eastland fight like [explicative] on civil rights and then go have lunch together, down in the Senate dining room. John wanted to see "regular order" writ large. Get to know one another. You know, John and I were both amused and I think Lindsey was at one of these events where John and I received two prestigious awards where the last year I was vice president and one immediately after, for our dignity and respect we showed to one another, we received an award for civility in public life. Allegheny College puts out this award every year for bipartisanship. John and I looked at each and said, 'What the [heck] is going on here?' No, not a joke. I said to Senator Flake, that's how it's supposed to be. We get an award? I'm serious. Think about this. Getting an award for your civility. Getting an award for bipartisanship. Classic John, Allegheny College, hundreds of people, got the award, and the Senate was in session. He spoke first and, as he walked off the stage and I walked on, he said, Joe, don't take it personally, but I don't want to hear what the [heck] you have to say, and left.

"One of John's major campaign people is now with the senate with the governor of Ohio, was on [TV] this morning and I happened to watch it. He said that Biden and McCain had a strange relationship; they always seemed to have each other's back. Whenever I was in trouble, John was the first guy there. I hope I was there for him. We never hesitate to give each other advice. He would call me in the middle of the campaign, [and] he'd say, 'What the [heck] did you say that for? You just screwed up, Joe.' I'd occasionally call him.

"Look, I've been thinking this week about why John's death hit the country so hard. Yes, he was a long-serving senator with a remarkable record. Yes, he was a two-time presidential candidate who captured the support and imagination of the American people and, yes, John was a war hero, demonstrated extraordinary courage. I think of John and my son when I think of Ingersoll's words" When duty throws the gauntlet down to fate and honor scorns to compromise with death, that is heroism." Everybody knows that about John. But I don't think it fully explains why the country has been so taken by John's passing. I think it's something more intangible.

"I think it's because they knew John believed so deeply and so passionately in the soul of America. He made it easier for them to have confidence and faith in America. His faith in this nation's core values made them feel it more genuinely themselves. His conviction was that we, as a country, would never walk away from the sacrifice generations of Americans have made to defend liberty, freedom and dignity around the world. It made average Americans proud of themselves and their country. His belief, and it was deep, was that Americans can do anything, withstand anything, and achieve anything. It was unflagging and ultimately reassuring. This man believed that so strongly. His capacity that we truly are the world's last best hope, the beacon to the world. There are principles and ideals more than ourselves worth sacrificing for and if necessary, dying for. Americans saw how he lived his life that way, and they knew the truth of what he was saying. I just think he gave Americans confidence.

"John was a hero. His character, courage, honor, integrity. I think it is understated when they say optimism. That's what made John special. Made John a giant among all of us. In my view, John didn't believe that America's future and faith rested on heroes. We used to talk about, and he understood what I hope we all remember: heroes didn't build this country. Ordinary people being given half a chance are capable of doing extraordinary things, extraordinary things. John knew ordinary Americans understood each of us has a duty to defend, integrity, dignity and birthright of every child. He carried it. Good communities are built by thousands of acts of decency that Americans, as I speak today, show each other every single day [that] deep in the DNA of this nation's soul lies a flame that was lit over 200 years ago. Each of us carries with us and each one of us has the capacity, the responsibility, and we can screw up the courage to ensure it does not extinguish. There's a thousand little things that make us different.

"Bottom line was, I think John believed in us. I think he believed in the American people, not just all the preambles. He believed in the American people, all 325 million of us. Even though John is no longer with us, he left us clear instructions. 'Believe always in the promise and greatness of America because nothing is inevitable here.' Close to the last thing John said took the whole nation, as he knew he was about to depart. That's what he wanted America to understand—not to build his legacy; he wanted America reminded, to understand. I think John's legacy is going to continue to inspire and challenge generations of leaders as they step forward and John McCain's America is not over. It is hyperbole. It's not over. It's not close.

"Cindy, John owed so much of what he was to you. You were his ballast. When I was with you both, I could see how he looked at you. Jill is the one. When we were in Hawaii, we first met you there and he kept staring at you. Jill said, Go up and talk to her. Doug, Andy, Sydney, Meghan, Jack, Jimmy, Bridget, you may not have had your father as long as you would like, but you got from him everything you need to pursue your own dreams. To follow the course of your own spirit. You are a living legacy, not hyperbole. You are a living legacy and proof of John McCain's success.

"Now John is going to take his rightful place in a long line of extraordinary leaders in this nation's history, who in their time and in their way, stood for freedom and stood for liberty and have made the American story the most improbable and most hopeful and most enduring story on earth. I know John said he hoped he played a small part in that story. John, you did much more than that, my friend. To paraphrase Shakespeare, "We shall not see his like again."

FAREWELL STATEMENT FROM SENATOR JOHN McCAIN

Monday, August 27, 2018

Phoenix, Arizona – Rick Davis, Senator John McCain's former presidential campaign manager and a family spokesman, read the following farewell statement from Senator McCain at a press conference at the Arizona State Capitol in Phoenix, Arizona today:

"**M**y fellow Americans, whom I have gratefully served for sixty years, and especially my fellow Arizonans,

"Thank you for the privilege of serving you and for the rewarding life that service in uniform and in public office has allowed me to lead. I have tried to serve our country honorably. I have made mistakes, but I hope my love for America will be weighed favorably against them.

"I have often observed that I am the luckiest person on Earth. I feel that way even now as I prepare for the end of my life. I have loved my life, all of it. I have had experiences, adventures and friendships enough for ten satisfying lives, and I am so thankful. Like most people, I have regrets. But I would not trade a day of my life, in good or bad times, for the best day of anyone else's.

"I owe that satisfaction to the love of my family. No man ever had a more loving wife or children he was prouder of than I am of mine. And I owe it to America. To be connected to America's causes—liberty, equal justice, respect for the dignity of all people—brings happiness more sublime than life's fleeting pleasures. Our identities and sense of worth are not circumscribed but enlarged by serving good causes bigger than ourselves.

"'Fellow Americans'—that association has meant more to me than any other. I lived and died a proud American. We are citizens of the world's greatest republic, a nation of ideals, not blood and soil. We are blessed and are a blessing to humanity when we uphold and advance those ideals at home and in the world. We have helped liberate more people from tyranny and poverty than ever before in history. We have acquired great wealth and power in the process.

"We weaken our greatness when we confuse our patriotism with tribal rivalries that have sown resentment and hatred and violence in all the corners of the globe. We weaken it when we hide behind walls, rather than tear them down, when we doubt the power of our ideals, rather than trust them to be the great force for change they have always been.

"We are three-hundred-and-twenty-five million opinionated, vociferous individuals. We argue and compete and sometimes even vilify each other in our raucous public debates. But we have always had so much more in common with each other than in disagreement. If only we remember that and give each other the benefit of the presumption that we all love our country, we will get through these challenging times. We will come through them stronger than before. We always do.

"Ten years ago, I had the privilege to concede defeat in the election for president. I want to end my farewell to you with the heartfelt faith in Americans that I felt so powerfully that evening.

"I feel it powerfully still.

"Do not despair of our present difficulties but believe always in the promise and greatness of America, because nothing is inevitable here. Americans never quit. We never surrender. We never hide from history. We make history.

"Farewell, fellow Americans. God bless you, and God bless America."

Endnotes

1   2022 Edelman Trust Barometer. 24 Jan. 2022, https://www.
    edelman.com/trust/2022-trust-barometer.

2   Carlson, John. Biden's Inaugural Speech Called for Ameri-
    cans to Embrace Civil Religion. What Does That Mean?, 20
    Jan. 2021, https://www.nbcnews.com/think/opinion/biden-s-
    inaugural-speech-called-americans-embrace-civil-religion-
    what-ncna1255084.

3   Friedman, Megan. Joe Biden Gave an Incredibly Powerful
    Speech at John McCain's Memorial. 30 Aug. 2018, https://
    www.townandcountrymag.com/society/politics/a22877209/
    joe-biden-eulogy-john-mccain-memorial-full-transcript/.

4   Lee Rainie, S. K. A. A. P. (2019, July 22). Trust and distrust
    in America. Pew Research Center - U.S. Politics & Policy.
    Retrieved July 13, 2022, from https://www.pewresearch.org/
    politics/2019/07/22/trust-and-distrust-in-america/

5   Affordable Care Act (ACA) - Glossary | HealthCare.gov,
    https://www.healthcare.gov/glossary/affordable-care-act/.

6   Public Trust in Government 1958-2021, https://www.
    pewresearch.org/politics/2022/06/06/public-trust-in-govern-
    ment-1958-2022/.

7 Blake, Aaron, and Eugene Scott. Joe Biden's Inauguration Speech, Annotated. 20 Jan. 2021, https://www.washingtonpost. com/politics/interactive/2021/01/20/biden-inauguration-speech/.

8 Reuters/Ipsos Poll: Biden's First 100 Days. ,https://www. ipsos.com/sites/default/files/ct/news/documents/2021-05/ Reuters%20Ipsos%20Large%20Issue%20Poll%20%232%20 Topline%20%20Write-up%20-%20Biden%20100%20 Days%20-%2012%20April%20thru%2016%20April%20 2021.pdf.

9 McNamara, Audrey. Romney: McConnell Said Electoral Vote Count Will Be "the Most Consequential Vote", 2 Jan. 2021, https://www.cbsnews.com/news/mitch-mcconnell-electoral-college-vote-most-consequential-mitt-romney/.

10 RMPBS PRESENTS...Divided We Fall: Unity Without Tragedy, 30 Apr. 2020, https://video.rmpbs.org/video/divided-we-fall-unity-without-tragedy-8pxtqc/.

11 Florida, Richard. How the 'Big Sort' Is Driving Political Polarization, 25 Oct. 2016, https://www.bloomberg.com/news/ articles/2016-10-25/how-the-big-sort-is-driving-political-polarization.

12 Battleground Poll. New Poll: Voters Rate Political Division As Top Issue Facing the Country. 15 June 2021, https://politics. georgetown.edu/2021/06/15/new-poll-georgetown-institute-of-politics-and-public-service-releases-june-2021-battleground-poll/.

13 Fueling the Fire: How Social Media Intensifies U.S. Political Polarization—And What Can Be Done About It, 13 Sept. 2021, https://www.stern.nyu.edu/experience-stern/faculty-research/fueling-fire-how-social-media-intensifies-u-s-political-polarization-and-what-can-be-done-about-it.

14 Solender, Andrew. Marjorie Taylor Greene Raises $3.2 Million In First Three Months Of 2021, 7 Apr. 2021, https://www.forbes.com/sites/andrewsolender/2021/04/07/marjorie-taylor-greene-raises-32-million-in-first-three-months-of-2021/?sh=75b7a1eb3d32.

15 Slisco, Aila. 'Grotesque, Dangerous': AOC, Omar Lead Dems in Slamming Paul Gosar Over Violent Anime Video. 8 Nov. 2021, https://www.newsweek.com/grotesque-dangerous-aoc-omar-lead-dems-slamming-paul-gosar-over-violent-anime-video-1647231.

16 Lungariello, Mark. Rep. Paul Gosar Doubles down on AOC, Biden Attack Video. 9 Nov. 2021, https://nypost.com/2021/11/09/rep-paul-gosar-doubles-down-on-aoc-biden-attack-video/.

17 Fulwood, Sam. Rep. Waters Labels Bush 'a Racist,' Endorses Clinton. 9 July 1992, https://www.latimes.com/archives/la-xpm-1992-07-09-mn-2366-story.html.

18 Phillips, John. Chief Trump Tormenter Maxine Waters Once Alleged the CIA Dumped Drugs into America's Cities. 1 Aug. 2018, https://www.ocregister.com/2018/08/01/chief-trump-tormenter-maxine-waters-once-alleged-the-cia-dumped-drugs-into-americas-cities/.

19 Ehrlich, Jamie. Maxine Waters Encourages Supporters to Harass Trump Administration Officials. 25 June 2018, https://www.cnn.com/2018/06/25/politics/maxine-waters-trump-officials/index.html.

20 Allen, Jonathan. Grayson: GOP Wants "'You to Die.'" 29 Sept. 2009, https://www.politico.com/story/2009/09/grayson-gop-wants-you-to-die-027726.

21 Schelenz, Robyn. Why Negative Campaigning Works—and How to Fight It. 12 Sept. 2019, https://www. universityofcalifornia.edu/news/why-negative-campaigning-works-and-how-fight-it#:~:text=Ledgerwood%20and%20 her%20colleagues%20have,still%20think%20it's%20a%20bust.

22 ADAMS, SAMUEL – Sermons and Biblical Studies, Biblia. work, https://www.biblia.work/sermons/adamssamuel/.

23 Cillizza, Chris. The Fix - The Best (Positive) Campaign Ad of the Cycle?, 23 Aug. 2010, http://voices.washingtonpost.com/ thefix/governors/the-best-positive-campaign-ad.html.

24 Pete's Rules of the Road, Democracy In Action, 2020, https:// www.democracyinaction.us/2020/buttigieg/buttigiegrules.html.

25 Berg, Joel. All You Can Eat: How Hungry Is America? Seven Stories Press, 2008.

26 Algeo, Matthew. All This Marvelous Potential Robert Kennedy's 1968 Tour of Appalachia. Chicago Review Press, 2020.

27 American Rhetoric: Robert F. Kennedy - Law Day Address at the University of Georgia Law School, https://www. americanrhetoric.com/speeches/rfkgeorgialawschool.htm.

28 Conant, Ed. Members of Congress Finally Doing What They're Supposed to Do. 4 Aug. 2013, https://www.nolabels. org/members-of-congress-finally-doing-what-theyre-supposed-to-do/.

29 Gottheimer, Josh, and Tom Reed. Let's Stop the Bickering and Fix the Health Care System, 4 Aug. 2017, https://www. nytimes.com/2017/08/04/opinion/bipartisan-health-care-reform.html.

30 Russakoff, Dale. 1997 Law Speeds Foster Children Adoption. 18 Jan. 1998, https://www.washingtonpost.com/wp-srv/ national/daily/april99/fosterlaw011898.htm.

31 Weisman , Jonathan, and Jennifer Steinhauer. Senate Women Lead in Effort to Find Accord. 14 Oct. 2013, https://www. nytimes.com/2013/10/15/us/senate-women-lead-in-effort-to-find-accord.html.

32 Rosenthal, Jack. Angry Ethnic Voices Decry a 'Racist and Dullard.' 17 June 1970, https://www.nytimes.com/1970/06/17/archives/angry-ethnic-voices-decry-a-racist-and-dullard-image.html.

33 Weisman , Jonathan, and Jennifer Steinhauer. Senate Women Lead in Effort to Find Accord. 14 Oct. 2013, https://www. nytimes.com/2013/10/15/us/senate-women-lead-in-effort-to-find-accord.html.

34 America in One Room. 19 Sept. 2019, https://cdd.stanford. edu/2019/america-in-one-room/.

35 Quinto, Richard, and Carter Dougherty. New Bipartisan Poll Shows Strong Support for Student Loan Debt Cancellation During COVID-19 Pandemic. 12 May 2020, https:// www.responsiblelending.org/media/new-bipartisan-poll-shows-strong-support-student-loan-debt-cancellation-during-covid-19.

36 Hern, Alex. Tim Berners-Lee on 30 Years of the World Wide Web: "We Can Get the Web We Want." 12 Mar. 2019, https:// www.theguardian.com/technology/2019/mar/12/tim-berners-lee-on-30-years-of-the-web-if-we-dream-a-little-we-can-get-the-web-we-want.

37 Amiri, Farnoush. The World Wide Web Is 30 Years Old—and Its Inventor Has a Warning for Us. 12 Mar. 2019, https://www. nbcnews.com/tech/tech-news/world-wide-web-30-its-inventor-has-warning-us-n982156.

38 Hern, Alex. Tim Berners-Lee on 30 Years of the World Wide Web: 'We Can Get the Web We Want." 12 Mar. 2019, https://www.theguardian.com/technology/2019/mar/12/tim-berners-lee-on-30-years-of-the-web-if-we-dream-a-little-we-can-get-the-web-we-want.

39 "America United": Finding Common Ground | JFK Library. https://www.jfklibrary.org/events-and-awards/forums/05-04-america-united.

40 Horowitz, Jeff, and Deepa Seetharaman. Facebook Executives Shut Down Efforts to Make the Site Less Divisive. 26 May 2020, https://www.wsj.com/articles/facebook-knows-it-encourages-division-top-executives-nixed-solutions-11590507499.

41 47 U.S. Code § 230 - Protection for Private Blocking and Screening of Offensive Material. https://www.law.cornell.edu/uscode/text/47/230.

42 Chuck Grassley: Big Tech Must Stop Censoring Americans, 12 Apr. 2021, https://iowatorch.com/2021/04/12/chuck-grassley-big-tech-must-stop-censoring-americans/.

43 Allyn, Bobby. What The Ruling In The Epic Games V. Apple Lawsuit Means For IPhone Users, 10 Sept. 2021, https://www.npr.org/2021/09/10/1036043886/apple-fortnite-epic-games-ruling-explained.

44 Chuck Grassley: Big Tech Must Stop Censoring Americans, 12 Apr. 2021, https://iowatorch.com/2021/04/12/chuck-grassley-big-tech-must-stop-censoring-americans/.

45 Walter Cronkite Quote: Our Job Is Only to Hold up the Mirror..., AZ Quotes, https://www.azquotes.com/quote/1057306.

46 Berry, Jeffrey M, and Sarah Sobieraj. *The Outrage Industry: Political Opinion Media and the New Incivility.* 1st ed., Oxford University Press, 2014.

47 Molyneux, Logan, and Mark Coddington. Aggregation, Clickbait and Their Effect on Perceptions of Journalistic Credibility and Quality, 16 June 2019, https://scholarshare.temple.edu/handle/20.500.12613/393.

48 Homepage. Center for Media Engagement. (2022, April 27). https://mediaengagement.org/

49 Hawkins, Stephen, et al. Hidden Tribes: A Study of America's Polarized Landscape. Oct. 2018, https://hiddentribes.us/media/qfpekz4g/hidden_tribes_report.pdf.

50 Why Stephen Fry Is Arguing against Political Correctness, with Jordan Peterson, 17 May 2018, https://www.cbc.ca/news/canada/toronto/stephen-fry-political-correctness-1.4662626.

51 Lee, Chisun, et al. Secret Spending in the States. 26 June 2016, https://www.brennancenter.org/our-work/research-reports/secret-spending-states.

52 Citizens United v. Federal Election Comm'n. Cornell Law School, 21 Jan. 2010, https://www.law.cornell.edu/supct/html/08-205.ZO.html.

53 Evers-HIllstrom, Karl. More Money, Less Transparency: A Decade under Citizens United. 14 Jan. 2020, https://www.opensecrets.org/news/reports/a-decade-under-citizens-united.

54 Most expensive ever: 2020 election cost $14.4 billion. OpenSecrets News. (2021, February 11). Retrieved July 13, 2022, from https://www.opensecrets.org/news/2021/02/2020-cycle-cost-14p4-billion-doubling-16/

55 Public Financing of Campaigns: Overview. National Conference of State Legislatures, 8 Feb. 2019, https://www.ncsl.org/research/elections-and-campaigns/public-financing-of-campaigns-overview.aspx.

56 The Honest Ads Act - Mark R. Warner, May 2019, https://www.warner.senate.gov/public/index.cfm/the-honest-ads-act.

57 Rothwell, Jonathan, and Christos Makridis. Politics Is Wrecking America's Pandemic Response. 17 Sept. 2020, https://www.brookings.edu/blog/up-front/2020/09/17/politics-is-wrecking-americas-pandemic-response/.

58 Clinton Colmenares, Director of News and Media Strategy. Why Has COVID and the Response to COVID Become So Political?, 9 Sept. 2021, https://news.furman.edu/2021/09/09/why-has-covid-and-the-response-to-covid-become-so-political/.

59 Lopez, German. How Political Polarization Broke America's Vaccine Campaign. 6 July 2021, https://www.vox.com/2021/7/6/22554198/political-polarization-vaccine-covid-19-coronavirus.

60 Part of a message from American naval officer Oliver Hazard Perry in 1813 after defeating and capturing Royal Navy ships in the Battle of Lake Erie.

61 Spetalnick, M. (2008, October 13). Republican anger bubbles up at McCain Rally. Reuters., from https://www.reuters.com/article/sppage014-n10414512-oistl/republican-anger-bubbles-up-at-mccain-rally-idUSN1041451220081013

62 Pramuk, Jacob. John McCain, in Final Message before Death, Says 'Do Not Despair of Our Present Difficulties' . 27 Aug. 2018, https://www.cnbc.com/2018/08/27/john-mccain-in-final-message-before-death-says-do-not-despair-of-our-present-difficulties.html.

A free ebook edition is available with the purchase of this book.

To claim your free ebook edition:

1. Visit MorganJamesBOGO.com
2. Sign your name CLEARLY in the space
3. Complete the form and submit a photo of the entire copyright page
4. You or your friend can download the ebook to your preferred device

Print & Digital Together Forever.

Snap a photo

Free ebook

Read anywhere